# Miscellaneous

*taking back your time selling on eBay*

ANNA PACKER

Miscellaneous:
Taking Back Your Time Selling On eBay

Copyright © 2020 by Anna Packer

ISBN 978-1-7337948-2-4

Published by Baltika Press
www.baltikapress.com

Edited by Doug Dennison.
Cover design by John Packer.

Printed in the United States of America.

*To John,*
*for sacrificing most of*
*your half of the garage*
*to the empire.*
*I love you.*

# ACKNOWLEDGEMENTS

*The Scavenger Life:*

*First and foremost, Jay and Ryanne! I literally would not and could not have built the life I have now without your kind example and virtual camaraderie. To the rest of the Scavenger Life community who tune in, call in, share with, and learn from each other: you guys are awesome! I love this community!*

*Thank you so much!*

# CONTENTS

GIL & ANYA GILDNER

# INTRODUCTION

The official name of my eBay store is Annaesthetic Miscellany. Annaesthetic is just a silly play on my name, but Miscellany has more intrigue. It immediately presents a riddle: how is this word pronounced? MISS-uh-lain-ee. miss-SELL-uh-nee. Sure, yeah. One of those two, probably. For all I knew, there could have been a third option. The pronunciation never mattered much to me though, because for a long time, I didn't really talk about my store. At least, not at first, and never by name. In the beginning, I built it silently—on a kind of self-imposed dare. I didn't anticipate ever having to say the name of the store; I named it that because, well, the items I was selling were (and still are) rather miscellaneous.

Of course, there did come a day when I needed to say the name. I had casually mentioned my store as my latest project, and my Dad wanted to look it up on eBay, just to check it out. Naturally, he asked what it was called. So I told him, Annaesthetic MISS-uh-lain-ee. His face kind of screwed up. His eyebrows twitched a little. "You mean, miss-SELL-uh-nee." I'm not sure whether it was a statement or a question, but I nodded and said something like, "um, sure, yeah." I was admittedly a little embarrassed; after all, who doesn't know how to say the name of her own store? Not to mention, who would totally wing it like that in front of her dad—not just any dad, but one who happens to be a career editor and critic of the English language in all forms. We all know who, at this point.

Seriously though, that moment of clumsily naming my store out loud to my dad is an excellent metaphor of this whole process: not totally knowing what I'm doing, but loving the idea enough to just jump in and get started, to wing it, to throw some spaghetti out into the universe and see what happens.

The funny thing is, in preparing to write this book, I actually looked up *miscellany* and discovered something—of course, my dad the editor wasn't wrong; miss-SELL-uh-nee is the British English pronunciation, and MISS-uh-lain-ee is the American English pronunciation. If you'll bear with me, I can't help but notice that a second lesson is tucked into this word that has come to characterize so much for me: there is more than one right way to say this word. Are there wrong ways? To be sure. But there are *multiple right ways*. My dad and I had two variations of this word rolling off our tongues, and somehow, we were actually both right—or at least, both not wrong. Our pronunciations sounded different, but there was no mistake. Both were equally valid, equally meaningful. As in many lessons of language, a broader moral shines through: there is more than one right way to orchestrate a miscellaneous life. Put a pin in that one.

I genuinely feel like this book happened to me. I love to write —songs, music, musical theater, play scripts, screenplays, poems—so somewhere inside, I always figured I'd write a book about something eventually. I mean, it's a lot of words and a lot of hard work—both things I love. I love projects. I love creating. I love making connections among seemingly disparate things.

Speaking of seemingly disparate things, what is this book about, anyway? Is it a memoir, or a how-to? Yes. This book has a dual purpose. One part is simply to document my experiences in the world of running my eBay business—including favorite stories and moments along the way while I still remember all the juicy details. The other part is to pull back the curtain for a full view of the realm behind the scenes and life beyond the practical processes of running the store.

I'm sharing my real-life (read: imperfect) story in hopes of encouraging inner sparks of creativity or innovation or motivation for anyone who relates to part of my own experience—from a love of thrifting, to a desperate desire to wriggle out of the choke hold of student loan debt, to seeking a fun financial runway for artistic projects. I *know* this kind of encouragement is important and effective; the only reason running an eBay store in this particular way occurred to me in the first place is because of two people doing that exact kind of personal, specific, transparent sharing of their own stories on a free and widely accessible podcast, *The Scavenger Life*. Hearing from others who already figured a bunch of this stuff out was how I became aware, courageous and curious enough to try it, and eventually, proficient in running my own store on my own terms. I do realize that if you peered into my garage, at first glance, you might think I'm a hoarder, and when you hear how little I'm willing to pay for a pair of shoes, you might think I'm stingy. However, the truth is, our world runs on generosity, abundance, and sharing what we have with each other—our methods, our experiences, our failures, our successes, and ourselves. I want to contribute; that's the bottom-line function of the book.

This is not a story of getting rich. If you live in Soho or SoCal, my numbers might not make sense to you. They make sense for me, my lifestyle, my cost of living, my phase of life, my bills, my priorities, my circumstances. It's not an exact roadmap for anyone else to follow to the penny; we all have to find our own way. While this book is definitely about my eBay store, that's hardly the sum of it. My life has changed drastically, and I have grown tremendously in tandem with my store. I would be remiss to leave out that side of the story—so I won't! You'll get a 360 view of this adventure, past, present, and future, in all its miscellaneous glory.

- I'm going to tell you all about:
- How and why I set up an official eBay store
- Where I find inventory and what kinds of things I sell
- The rules I follow to stay organized and keep growing
- My storage situation and system
- The overall process for any given item, from sourcing to shipping, including the many micro-processes peppered throughout
- The costs associated with running my store, financial and otherwise
- The benefits associated with running my store, financial and otherwise
- The miscellaneous life I now thoroughly enjoy and so many things I've learned along the way

I'm providing actual numbers (and charts!) throughout the book because having access to a transparent example is what helped me the most. Also, there is a lot of data associated with this story, and I'm kind of a data nerd—*kind of*—I've got nothing on actual math people, and I know it. Even so, in my opinion, the data is a vital element of any representation of my store; you may not feel the same way, and that's alright. You can take or leave the data behind the story, but trust me, you don't want to miss the story behind the data.

ANNA PACKER

# THE BEGINNING

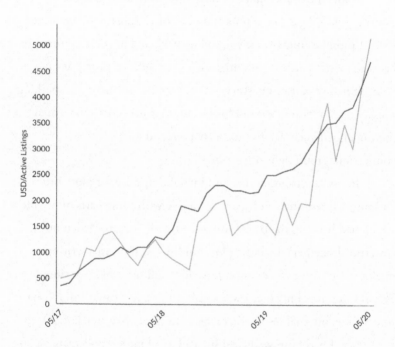

*How did you get into this?*

# CHAPTER 1: OFF THE GROUND

Allow me to introduce myself with a little background information. I'll get to the nuts and bolts of running my eBay store soon, I promise. But I want you to know where I'm coming from, because there's a chance you might relate to some of it. If you can see yourself in any part of my story—past, present, or future—something might click for you like it did for me, and I don't want you to miss out on a good click. So give me a chapter, and look for the connections. You might be surprised.

In my late twenties, I found myself desperate for more time and internal resources and space to engage with some parts of my life which had been on the back burner for far too long (or fallen off the stovetop altogether), including but not limited to music, writing, quality time with people I love, traveling, and plain old free time. When I examined my life, I was crushed to discover that I didn't have much time, internal resources, or space to spare. Not much *at all*.

See, I had borrowed (and spent) lots of money and years on an education in clinical counseling psychology and criminal justice, working mostly as a Licensed Professional Counselor in private practice and teaching undergraduate psychology classes. On the whole, I loved that work; it just wasn't enough to make my life feel the kind of full I always desired. I was busy! And I was helping people! But I realized counseling and teaching psychology as the main pillars of my work life did not equal an ideal fit for me. It wasn't sustainable, and once I knew that, I couldn't un-know it. Yikes.

So, with some pretty serious emotional turmoil, I started trying stuff with the scant spare time I did have. I tried to identify what wasn't working and to make room to figure out what would work. Music is a lifelong passion of mine, and I was missing it so much, it hurt. I crowbarred some music back into my life; I started dreaming again. That all began about four years ago. Cut to now—I run a very miscellaneous online store selling second-hand stuff, among (many) other things. Did I see that coming? Not exactly.

My adventure in eBay is an organized-but-somehow-still-messy metaphor for my whole life, and it's still relatively new for me. Running the store as my main source of income is the result of a fairly recent transition, so I naturally thought this would be a great point in the process to take inventory (ha!) of what this transition means for my life, examining my processes and my real numbers— the bottom line—and beyond.

I'm not interested in waiting until I've arrived at some pinnacle to share my story. I don't currently have a lot of clarity about what that pinnacle would be, and I have a sneaking suspicion that we never really arrive, anyway. That's not to say we never reach our goals; it's just that we're never done creating new ones. Many people tell their stories from the finish line. There's nothing wrong with that, but I'm often more compelled by stories of people in the middle—probably because I am one of those people.

I haven't exactly conducted market research, but I have been surprised over and over at how frequently and extensively I find myself discussing my eBay store—with anyone, with everyone. At weddings and parties, at church, at my former office, at home, at friends' homes, at Christmas, on vacation, with family, with strangers, on beaches, on mountains, in coffee shops, in Target (hi, I love you). I don't mean to sound like a Dr. Seuss book, nor imply that I literally never shut up about my store. The reason I find myself talking about it so much is that *people are always asking me about it.* All. Ways. Follow-up questions galore, *ad nauseam* even. The ins, the outs, the logistics, the philosophy.

People are fascinated by this world of selling second-hand stuff online, regardless of how well they know me personally. In fact, I think most of their interest has very little if anything to do with me— and that's fair. I think that's super cool, actually, because I am convinced that most people could do this kind of thing; there is nothing special about me. That's good news for everybody. I decided to write all of this down so I could just chuck a book at the next person who asks me this inevitable series of questions. Just kidding. I decided to write it all down in hopes of providing useful, encouraging information for others. Plus, it's fun. This whole miscellaneous world is fun, and writing a book about it is no exception.

## A FREE EDUCATION

Let's enter the story around the time I heard about other people actually making an honest-to-goodness living on eBay. (Don't worry, there is plenty that happened before that, but I'm saving some sordid details for later.) It was sometime in 2016. I had begun educating myself on personal finance, and had found this awesome podcast called *The Afford Anything Podcast*, hosted by Paula Pant. She has single handedly educated me so much, it's not even funny, and I still love listening to her podcast to this day. Many of her episodes are interviews with people who share experience and insight to help others become financially independent, debt free, and more financially literate. So good.

The eleventh episode of *Afford Anything* was an interview with this delightful duo, Jay and Ryanne, who host *The Scavenger Life Podcast* (and an amazing online community) all about their eBay store. I was fascinated by their story, and immediately subscribed to *The Scavenger Life Podcast*, too. In my "free" time (driving, cleaning my house, cooking, exercising, showering, you name it) I binge-listened to as many episodes as I could as quickly as I could, like a busy little sponge soaking up every detail about how they used an eBay store as the cornerstone of a frugal, entrepreneurial lifestyle.

I had bought much on eBay over the years, from media to cool bookends to the pearl necklaces my bridesmaids wore at my wedding. I had even sold a few things on eBay, mostly for fun or a little extra cash (buh-bye, old textbooks), but I had never considered or specifically heard about anybody running a full-time business on eBay the way Jay and Ryanne were—and obviously, it was working! On *The Scavenger Life Podcast*, they weren't telling anyone how to make a million dollars or sharing ten secret steps to that elusive passive income so many are after; they were simply giving real numbers and real experiences from their week-to-week life of running their store. They talked about sweat equity, instinct, and deferred income (as opposed to passive income). They talked about frugality. I'm not gonna lie, I kind of fell in love.

Without their weekly encouragement and transparency, I never would have realized what was possible for me, and I certainly would never have found myself writing this book. Let me make it abundantly clear: many of these practical ideas and strategies and

ANNA PACKER

methods involved in the way I run my store are directly influenced by their example. Sometimes I didn't reinvent the wheel, sometimes I figured out my own way. That combination works well for me. I do my best to give credit where it's due, and the *Scavenger Life* creators (and community) deserve a *lot* of credit. In fact, if you read this book and decide to experiment with running your own eBay store, I urge you to binge listen to every *Scavenger Life Podcast* episode, as I did. They have created an amazing community, and I was able to get an education from them with no money in little time—enough to start a business that stands, this year, to generate the most income I've ever made in a year. Ironically, it seems the free education will be what ultimately pays the bill for my two bachelor's degrees and one master's degree—and I'm not even mad about it.

So, I found the *Scavenger Life*. Or it found me. I listened; I learned. I could actually see myself trying out something similar to what Jay and Ryanne had created. I was anxious that my husband, John, might think I was doing a poorly-disguised swan dive into hoarding, so I took a cartoony gulp and explained to him why I was rifling through all of our stuff to do an eBay experiment. (He, of course, was chill about it.)

This is *not* a story of taking an exhilarating leap into the unknown, trusting the net would appear to catch me. I love those stories. But this story is more about curiosity, being slow and consistent-ish, and most importantly, being open to the possibilities. I used what I already had. I had officially decided to start this store shortly after I had taken a carload of stuff to Goodwill, so I was kicking myself, thinking I surely didn't have anything else to clean out . . . but I *opened my eyes and looked* and found about 100 items

20

around my house that were less important to me than giving this thing a try. That really is all it takes to start.

In mid-May 2017, I listed a whole bunch of things—rapidly—and pretty soon things started selling. The 140th item I listed, a miniature collectible tea set, was my third-ever sale; it sold the day I listed it, for over a hundred bucks—more than 10 times what I paid for it. Lightbulb. Suddenly, this thing seemed plausible—but before long, that lightbulb feeling gave way to the old familiar self doubt and low-grade anxiety that accompanies doing something new or scary, including starting a business from scratch. So I felt it, acknowledged it, and kept listing.

By the end of my first month, I had sold 19 out of 280 items listed and profited about $300. For the first of many, many times, I asked myself: is this working? Maybe. Keep experimenting.

## ALL IN

A lot of life happened from May 2017 to January 2019. I started this eBay store on the side, as an experiment; in fact, for the first couple of years, I wasn't particularly aiming to make it the full-time gig it is today. However, I was having a blast. My garage became my shipping station and inventory warehouse. Honestly, I was having a blast! And actually, I was making real money. After five months of consistent-ish listing, in October 2017, I made more than $500 in a month for the first time. I kept listing. In October 2018, I made more than $1,000 in a month for the first time. The bigger the eBay store got, the more I was able to scale back my counseling practice, which alleviated a lot of my burnout. The inventory went up and my caseload went down. It wasn't a 1-for-1 exchange, though. I had more time. More emotional bandwidth. More music in my life. It was getting better.

January 2019, I realized it still wasn't enough. Tragedy smashed into my atmosphere, wrecking my family. John and I got a call on a Monday in the early part of January from my mom; my Aunt Patti had suffered a severe brain bleed while hospitalized for cancer treatment, and she wasn't expected to live through the night. John and I (and our two cats, Cinder and Dobby) live 600 miles from my family, so we knew there was no way we could make it to Patti in time. So we cried, prayed, periodically attempted to sleep, and checked our phones compulsively for the dreaded call or text.

But against all odds, Patti lived through the night. So we jumped in the car early Tuesday and cried and prayed our way across the 600 miles to the hospital in St. Louis. Literally on the way, I cancelled all my therapy sessions with clients for the week, extended my handling time in the eBay store, and didn't give a single thought to how I'd cover my bills. It just didn't matter. That phone call had begun what turned out to be easily the most hellacious weeks of my life—day in and day out in intensive care and cancer treatment units.

I could write a whole book about the gravity of the dream-world of miracles and tragedies we lived in, holding our breath for three weeks while Patti fought for her life, in some of the most bizarre circumstances imaginable. When we made it to St. Louis, we got to see her. To touch her. To pray over her. To talk to her while she was still unconscious in ICU. Days turned into a week; she stayed with us, so I cancelled my sessions for the next week and stayed in St. Louis. John drove home for the second week to take care of some things back at home and at his job. Again, she stayed, so I stayed, cancelling a third consecutive full week of therapy sessions with my clients. John drove all the way back north for the third week, and at the end of that week, Patti died. She was 57. In a state of severe sadness, shock, and exhaustion, John and I drove back home a few days later. It was unbelievable.

I had been gone for three weeks. I hadn't been in a therapy session in almost a month, and now I was consumed by the most devastating, disorienting loss I'd ever experienced. Patti wasn't just my aunt. She was my soul sister, godmother, confidant, and lifelong best friend. Our birthdays were a day apart—we almost always celebrated together. My whole childhood, I kicked myself for not being born a day later, because my mom always teased me that I'd have been sent to live with her if I'd been born on her birthday.

In fact, for the couple of years preceding her sudden death, I'd been dreaming of moving back north, in part so I could spend more of my life with her again. A couple times a year was not enough; it never had been. I absolutely loved spending time with her. My whole life, she'd be my knight in shining blue Honda every weekend she could, picking me up for a weekend of "bumming around" (which closely approximates my experience of thrift shopping now—thrifting, yardsaling, clearance-rack picking, etc.), watching Elvis movies and Bridgette Jones, and making silly crafts. We'd listen to music, eat frozen pizza, and laugh until we cried.

I will forever treasure my rich history with Patti, a treasury of memories I am so fortunate to have, but when I got home from St. Louis in January 2019, I almost could not function for losing her—her, and our whole future together—in one fell swoop. I needed room to grieve, but it was all I could do to "healthfully compartmentalize" my pain to be present with my clients, who had been so incredibly gracious to me when I needed to be out of town for a three-week emergency. I feel so grateful that I somehow had the capacity to do that while I was getting through the initial shock of loss, but I knew it was not a long-term solution. Not to mention, during those three weeks of absence from my private practice, my eBay store income covered the bills I normally would have covered with income from my therapy sessions. That alone sparked a sobering realization—like, wow, thank God I started that experiment a year and a half ago. I would have been dealing with a whole other layer of problems (or taking a big chunk out of my savings) had the store not been whirring away in the background.

I already knew, arriving back home after three weeks in hell with the worst finale imaginable, I'd be going back up north for another week, at least. Patti's older sister, my Aunt Cindy, and I had decided we would both make the trek back home (her from the west coast, me from the east) to team up and help my mom and grandfather deal with all the aftermath of Patti's death—closing accounts, sorting through her belongings, organizing things for memorial services in the future, and a million other tasks that fall under the "aftermath" umbrella. Many things compelled me to participate in this aftermath, as you might imagine, and I was very grateful that, thanks to my awesome husband and my eBay store, I could *actually afford* to take the time to do it. Another whole week. If you're counting, that adds up to an entire month's worth of weeks, out of the first two months of the year that I was totally absent from my practice *and* not listing anything new. The performance of my eBay store, it seemed, was unaffected. Things kept selling consistently, just as they had been all along.

On a practical level, the eBay store had frankly impressed me and covered my bills when it was the last thing I had room to worry about. On a more existential level, as is often the case with profound loss, this whole experience made me think differently about my own life. It gave me a perspective I couldn't have accessed before. I still wanted to help other people, yes, but I also wanted to spend the days I've got on earth doing whatever is the highest and best use of myself, my time, and my unique gifts and talents. I did *not* want to spend the rest of my days lying in the bed I'd made for myself when I was a teenager (with a less-than-fully-developed prefrontal cortex, mind you). I just couldn't continue to cling to decisions and debts from back then out of sheer obligation, calling it responsibility. Lipstick on a pig, and all that. I couldn't keep fooling myself anymore. Sometime in early 2019, a bigger, brighter lightbulb began to glow: letting go of those past decisions and limitations and welcoming massive change *was* the most responsible thing I could do with my life.

# THE SOURCES

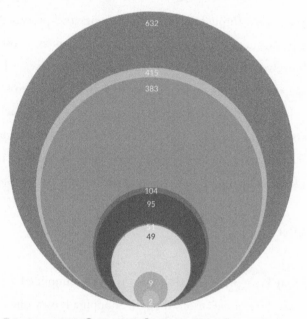

632

415
383

104
95

51
49

9

2

○ Consignment (2.82%) ● eBay (0.52%) ● Estate Sales (2.93%) ● Free (36.32%)
● Independent Thrift Shops (5.46%) ● For-Profit Thrift Shops (22.01%)
○ Nonprofit Chain Thrift Shops (23.85%) ● Retail Arbitrage (0.11%) ● Yardsales (5.98%)

*Where do you find stuff?*

# CHAPTER 2: ORIGINS

You made it through the backstory! Congrats. I promised you nuts and bolts, and they abound in the next few chapters. Most of them I borrowed or modified from others in the first place, as I got my store up and running on the side in early 2017. So, when it was time to take my store to the next level, I took a similar approach: see what's working and do more of it, better. One of the core concepts of my eBay store is keep on listing, no matter what. The thing is, in order to keep on listing you have to have stuff to list. About that . . .

## SHOPPING

To say I'm a professional shopper is an oversimplified, partial truth at best. It's not *too* far off, though. Shopping is only one part of the multi-process matrix of running a quirky little eBay resale business—but it's definitely one of the most fun parts. Rarely does drudgery creep in when I shop, or to use a more inclusive term, source. The vast majority of items in my store are sourced through some kind of shopping process, be it swiping my debit card at the thrift store, paying cash at a yardsale, or purchasing online with a few keystrokes. One of my favorite things about running my store is being able to treasure hunt in so many different environments—

there's really never a dull moment, and if I suspect that I might be about to encounter a dull moment, I can go shop someplace else.

However, shopping isn't the only avenue. Sometimes I don't pay anything for items—no, I am not talking about stealing. I find stuff that I can sell sometimes, like on the curb or sidewalk or free bin at the local buy-sell-trade bookstore. My family and friends simply give me stuff sometimes when they're cleaning out; when I declutter my own stuff, I usually harvest some new items for my store. Sure, that means those items move from a place in my actual house to a place in my garage, but they get out of my living space (and eventually turn a profit) all the same.

There are so many places to source items, I daresay especially for those of us who are scrappy and comfortable with creativity. Tangible treasure abounds in our world, in an incredibly and increasingly overwhelming way, in my experience. For example, long before I had an eBay store, back when I would sell things just occasionally, my step-mom had me list a couple of elaborately designed Christmas village pieces that sold for hundreds, which we split between us. Thanks, Trish! Guess where she found those Christmas village pieces, new in their boxes, unopened and virtually untouched? A *dumpster*. The fact that it's more "economical" for large retailers to literally trash brand new items than to, oh, I don't know, *sell them*, even donate them, or anything *but* toss them directly into a landfill, is beyond me. Lucky for planet earth, Trish, and me, these particular brand new items had been ditched in a dumpster that was legally diveable. I haven't sourced for my store via dumpster diving, but in the right conditions (read: legal and not covered in putrid waste of any kind) I'd probably go for it.

## ANYWHERE, EVERYWHERE

Here is a (kinda) exhaustive list of all the places I have sourced items so far:

- Local Buy-Sell-Trade Books & Media Store Free Bin (2nd & Charles, McKay's)
- Retail Outlet & Salvage Shops (Bargain Hunt, Dirt Cheap)
- Regular Retail Shops (Target, Walmart)
- Anthropologie (once: a clearance item)
- National & Regional Chain Thrift Stores (Goodwills, America's Thrift Stores, Value Village, Thrift Smart)
- Independent Thrift Stores (Granny's Garage Shop, Rockmart Thrift, This N That, Irene's Thrift, Rush Cheer, West VA Thrift, Florida Thrift, Southern Thrift, Family Shop Main Street)
- Thrift Store Outlets (Goodwill Outlet, Park Avenue Thrift Outlet)
- Charity Shops, Ministries, & Other Non-Profit Thrift Stores (Atlanta Mission, Episcopal Thrift, Gateway Thrift, Pier Foundation, Salvation Army, St. Vincent De Paul Society, Dallas First Choice, Main Street Mission Thrift Store, Peace Place, Island Thrift, Center of Hope, project safe, AL Escondido, Ayla's Acres, Mississippi Thrift, Nothing Wasted, St. Mary's Upscale Thrift)
- Craigslist (Once: a huge lot of fabric I bought to split with my friend who is a historical costume designer—Hi, Amanda!—She picked what she wanted and I sold off the rest to cover the cost of the whole lot! Talk about a win-win!)
- eBay (cannibalistic, I know—many different sellers)
- My Own Home (an embarrassing number of things)

- The Homes of Friends & Family Members (Thanks Mom, Leah, Jacob, MJ, Herschel, Trish, Doug, Theresa, Amanda, Patti, Cindy, Kim, Glen, Jer, Nicole, Katie, Kelly, Cristina, and John, just to name a few)
- Flea Markets (Marine Flea Market)
- Garage, Yard, Rummage, Estate, & Moving Sales (countless and not as well-documented)
- Store Closing Sales (Retail and thrift)
- Antique & Consignment Shops (Wheelin' & Dealin', Franklin's Antiques)
- Curbs & Sidewalks (box of super cool pint glasses in Atlanta near one of my favorite tattoo shops)

Now, I don't *always* go to *all* these sources; some I didn't have a stellar experience with, or I stopped in while traveling and probably will never go back because I won't be in that area again. I have sold items from every single place on the list, which are spread out across Georgia, Florida, West Virginia, Arkansas, California, Illinois, Missouri, Tennessee, Alabama, Mississippi. They are mostly in Georgia, where I currently live, and I certainly have my favorite Top 5, give or take, that are within an hour's drive of my home. My ideal sources meet the following criteria to some degree in no particular order: low cost, great quality items, convenient location, regular new inventory, reseller-friendly, charitable and volume-based business model. All of my favorites have some combination of most of those.

Having ideal places to source is great, but my sourcing experience fresh is fun and important, too. I love to revisit my favorite places over and over, but I'm definitely an opportunist at heart. I pop into new sources all the time (a thrift store I've never visited before, a yardsale that happens to be on my route, etc.) There is so much abundance everywhere, and I truly believe that for the small percentage of people who might make full-time work out of reselling, there is certainly room for all of us. Even so, to find good stuff, we all have to stay curious, flexible, willing to experiment, and even open to serendipity. Let me tell you a story about how that kind of approach pays off.

One of my favorite yardsales ever, I shopped one Saturday morning during the first summer I was building my eBay store. I went to a neighborhood-wide yardsale and stopped at a few houses; I honestly didn't find too much at first, but the last house I visited, a woman was selling her gorgeous vintage Burberry trench coat. It was seriously beautiful; and it was $20. It was unheard of for me to spend $20 on any one thing, not to mention all I had with me was a $20 bill, but I knew I had to get this coat. It actually fit me like a glove, and I seriously considered keeping it. When I confirmed I could sell it for several hundred dollars though, I decided to list it instead, and it did sell for around $250.

The coat itself was an incredible find, but the reason this was one of my favorite sourcing experiences actually happened later. I had used all of my cash to purchase the coat, so I went home to regroup. Later on, John and I went back to that same house together and bought a box containing a lifetime collection of vintage European postcards—the whole box was $5. We had so much fun hearing the stories of the family's travels from this perfect stranger and her husband, who were the sweetest people. We also had a blast looking through decades of beautiful postcards from all over Europe. I kept some of them, and I've sold many others. There were no hard feelings involved, either; the sellers were happy to clean out some of their extra stuff, and we were happy to purchase the postcards, connect with them, and hear their fun stories!

One of my more recently discovered sources has been a local online estate sale auction site that features online bidding with in-person pickup. It's been very interesting; all the bidding happens online based on photos, and then you pay for your items online and show up at a designated time to pick up your items. It's efficient, and I've been able to get some great stuff super cheap. The drawback is, all you have to work with are the photos, and some items may come across a little differently in person. Sometimes, things are worse for wear than they appeared to be in the photos, but sometimes there are hidden treasures to discover when you arrive for pick-up! Items may have other items hidden inside of them, or get lumped together with things other buyers have left behind. I became the proud owner (and seller) of a couple of huge Marlboro cigarette banners when I thought I was only purchasing a collection of 10 briefcases. It turned out to be 10 briefcases and two massive Marlboro banners for $5 total, and to date, three of those 12 items have sold, for a combined total of over $400. The morals of the story? There is often more than meets the eye, and there most assuredly is still treasure in the wild.

## CURBSIDE DESTINY

One of my favorite experiences of building this store with very little money and a lot of faith involved finding something on the curb at a thrift store! This actually happened. One morning, I was wrestling with a bunch of envelopes in the shipping area of my garage, where I stage the items that have been purchased and pack them for shipment. I was really struggling to get my mailing supplies organized; it's an ongoing struggle, actually. That day, I was extra frustrated because I felt like I needed some better infrastructure in this area, but I had given myself a tiny budget to reinvest into the store that week, and it was already going to be tight just getting a decent-sized haul of new items to list. I simply couldn't imagine having enough left over to purchase some kind of desktop organizer, nor could I imagine what kind of organizer might even work. I was flustered, so I said a quick prayer, asking God to provide me, somehow, an envelope organizer, ASAP please, and headed out to one of my favorite charity shops with my tiny budget. I parked behind the building and walked around to the front door—well, I almost made it to the front door, before nearly tripping on—you guessed it —an envelope sorter. It was a big, beautiful, beige dinosaur from the era of massive fax machines and perforated printer paper. Just sitting *outside* this shop with a "Free" sign on it. I almost cried. I scooped it up and carried it inside, asking the cashier if it was really, actually free. She giggled, delighted that I was so delighted to take it off her hands. She had set it outside about one minute before I pulled up to the shop. She explained that this fabulous, six-trayed sorter had been taking up precious real estate in their back room for years, and she had just maneuvered around it for the last time that morning, deciding it had to go, once and for all. I thanked her profusely, stashed it in my car, and returned to the shop to source inventory. I couldn't stop smiling the whole time I shopped. That envelope organizer is a mainstay of my shipping station to this day.

# CHAPTER 3: SHOPPING RULES

Since most things aren't actually free, I'm going to elaborate a little on how I make decisions related to purchasing inventory; I've got a few flexible rules to help keep me on track. Following these rules is more of an art than a science, and as you'll see, worthy exceptions aren't out of the question.

## TWO THUMBS, FOUR RULES

Who has two thumbs and likes to make rules? This girl. Okay, I definitely don't consider myself a rule person overall, because I'm a bit of a rebel at heart, but I *do* enjoy rules that help me stay frugal and focused, and simplify my decision making while I'm shopping for things to fill my store. I make better business decisions when my foundation is made up of objective criteria rather than feelings, though instincts and feelings are allowed a seat at the table. More on that later; this part is all about the objective stuff!

Some of these rules are wheels I didn't bother to reinvent, cobbled together from what many other resellers and folks in the Scavenger Life community do. Many of them have been tweaked over time, and all of them are fairly soft rules; after all, in the world of miscellany, there are plenty of exceptions.

I chose, developed, and continue to use and adapt these rules in order to prevent myself from getting overwhelmed with inventory, to keep overhead costs low and somewhat predictable, and to make the most out of my relatively small sourcing budget, which was especially tiny in the beginning. I use these rules in a continuous, experimental feedback loop, whether I am building my inventory numbers or maintaining at an intentional plateau. They're rules of thumb because they are designed for general use, based on experiential knowledge and practicality, and because I believe rules like these and thumbs should exist in roughly similar quantities; in other words, you shouldn't have too many more rules than what you can count on your thumbs. Too many rules clutter rather than clarify decision making. I'm definitely pushing it already; having four rules, I technically have to count my big toes, too. Alas, I digress. Let's get to 'em!

## RULE 1: SHOOT FOR UNDER $3 PER ITEM.

I generally won't spend more than $3 for an item, unless I am relatively certain it will sell for over $75. Were those numbers selected somewhat arbitrarily? Yes, but now that they have been established, the numbers themselves are clear and objective. I absolutely love getting things for under a dollar per item, and I am giddy if the average cost of goods for the whole shopping trip is under a dollar per item. I'm not playing around with this rule: my all-time average cost of goods is 80 cents per item.

If your main experience with buying secondhand items is going to your local Goodwill, that might sound crazy to you. I assure you, I am not crazy, and in fact, I am pretty serious about this rule. It's a reasonable rule for me, because I have found sources of store-worthy stuff that is consistently incredibly cheap and available. One of my favorite places to shop for clothes, a regional thrift store outlet (yes, that's a thing), has one day of *every single week* during which every item is 25 cents. That means I can get 80 items for my store for a little over 20 bucks after tax. Sure, I have to rake through hundreds or thousands of items over the course of a couple of hours to find 80 items that I deem store-worthy, but that's the fun part! Even if all of those items sold for $2.50 each, I'd be making $200 on that $20 investment. The items I choose will not, in fact, sell that cheaply though, because . . .

## RULE 2: ONLY BUY STUFF THAT WILL SELL FOR $20+ OR AT LEAST 10X WHAT I PAID FOR IT.

This one is definitely a flexible rule, because I don't meticulously research each item as I'm shopping. Even if I did, the market for any given item is subject to change. Also, some stuff might sell for $10 or $15, but it's free, so am I going to turn down three free items that might sell for a combined total of $40? Some days, yes; other days, no. One man's wildflower field is another man's weed patch, or something like that. The point is, it depends. You can see the ample room here for grey. Most items I source do cost some little bit of cash, but every single item, even the free ones, cost my time to process them. So, this rule kind of feeds into a little equation when I'm trying to decide whether to purchase an item or not: is this item worth at least $20 *plus* at least 20 minutes of my time to process it and get it listed and shipped after it sells, and if not, does it have some other redeeming quality making it worthy of a spot in my store? Ironically, the second part of this rule, *at least 10 times what I paid for it*, mostly applies to items I buy that break rule one. (I told you I'm not really a rule person.) I consider this rule when I pay more than $3 for an item, but I also consider this rule the whole time that item is for sale. For example, I bought a really cool black vinyl ski jacket for $12, hoping to sell it for over $120—and actually, it sold during the writing of this chapter for $120 plus shipping! I've gotten lower offers on this item in the past, but because of this rule, I didn't take them. I held out for the higher price, and in this case, sticking to the rule literally paid off!

## RULE 3: SOURCE STUFF I'M INTERESTED IN.

This one is simple. If it bores me to tears and won't certainly sell fast and for hundreds of dollars, I'll pass. Again, there is *so much stuff* out there, and running this store is what I spend a decent amount of my time (i.e. my life) doing. It's okay to pass on things. A great example of this is when the AC unit housed in my attic malfunctioned, and our trusty AC mechanic came out to diagnose it (this was not our first rodeo, unfortunately). He noticed all the stuff in my garage and was instantly curious about why I had so much stuff—I explained to him about the eBay store, and he immediately thought of all the AC components in his workshop which he had acquired over the years that could be sold secondhand for amazing prices online. He asked me if I'd be interested in consigning it for him in my shop, and after considering it, I encouraged him to set up his own store on eBay because it simply wasn't in my wheelhouse and

I knew in my heart that I wasn't really interested enough in those kinds of items to spend my time—arguably any person's most valuable resource—on processing those items. And you know what? I'm not worried at all that I'm missing out. There are plenty of things I am interested in—more than I can imagine or handle—out there for me to find and sell.

Another example is vintage matchbooks: those little packets of safety matches that seemingly every business used to give out as a cheap advertising tool throughout much of the last several decades. Some places still give them away. In many ways, they are ideal items to sell on eBay: they are neat and collectible, they can be purchased in enormous lots for dirt cheap online and elsewhere, they are easy to store and ship because they are tiny and lightweight, straightforward and quick to photograph, etc. I got into them by experiment, happening upon a cheap lot of about five hundred of them at an estate sale, and had a lot of fun sorting and listing them for a while. In fact, this was a fantastic way to build my inventory during the COVID-19 quarantine weeks, because I already had hundreds of them just waiting to be listed!

Pretty soon, I got burnt out on them (pun 100% intended). I was over it, for the time being; selling them to collectors is fun, but they move pretty slow and there are very particular guidelines for shipping them (they can't be transported on planes because they're flammable). It also just gets to be a real slog to list things that are almost exactly the same, one after another in rapid succession. I still have a box of unlisted matchbooks in my garage right now that I'm saving for a rainy day, another quarantine, or the next time the pickings are slim on a sourcing day. I'll keep listing them slowly, supplementing the stuff I'm just plain more interested in. I got them so cheap, I don't feel bad letting them sit a while.

## RULE 4: LEAN TIMES = 10% REINVESTED.

This rule is like the bumpers on my lane at a bowling alley. It keeps me from winding up in the gutter? Sort of; when I implement it, I don't get a huge backlog of inventory piling up in my garage and I don't overspend. My store grows in a stable proportion, and there is a clear boundary for how much I can afford to spend; I can keep a predetermined, appropriate budget in mind when I'm sourcing.

This is how I started out: reinvesting 10 percent of my profit into inventory. I leaned into being radically frugal with my store (which is different from just being cheap, thank you) because I wanted the best value possible and I never wanted to be in debt with my store for any reason. A huge impetus for starting this business in the first place was to pay off the student loan debt I already had.

John and I have both always worked full time and both incomes have always been necessary, so for this reason among others, it was never an option to just quit my job and soul-search for a while. The flip side, of course, is that being part of a two-income household meant that it also wasn't *all* on me. That was a crucial piece of the puzzle that allowed me to have the little bit of flexibility to experiment with this in the first place. In any case though, I needed to make money, and I'd been down a couple of other roads with side hustles that ultimately only broke even because of how much I had to continuously reinvest in them. With eBay, I needed to actually be able to keep some of my income right off the bat (shocking, I know). While it's totally reasonable and acceptable for many new businesses to not even turn a profit in their first year (or two or three or more), that never made sense to me for this business. It wasn't necessary, and in my mind, there was simply no appeal. I was already growing it as fast as I could as a one-monkey circus.

These days, I don't follow this rule the way I did in the beginning. Rather, I revert to this rule when I feel I need to balance my spending or I'm tight on cash flow for the month. This rule now operates on a switch of sorts. It used to be constantly switched on, then at some point I switched it off, and currently, I'm considering switching it back on—not out of necessity, but to challenge myself to get some higher-dollar items. Ten percent of my monthly profit now includes a lot more spending power than it did when I was starting out. That whole thing about it taking money to make money really does hold some water (unlike that $12 ski jacket I mentioned).

In summary, these four rules serve to ensure *very* low overhead cost for my store. If I suddenly catapult to rock stardom or get sick and tired of this business or totally abandon the Internet someday (I've certainly been tempted), I could donate every single item I have purchased back into circulation at my favorite thrift stores without batting an eye, knowing that for the hundreds I've paid, I've already made thousands and never once been in the red. In fact, so far I've made a little over 33x what I've invested into my inventory, and these rules have kept me focused and organized the whole time.

These are just four rules that have worked well for me, but there are countless variations of these and other rules altogether to consider. Four rules are plenty to keep me in line, but not so many that my inner rebel is tempted to abandon all semblance of order in favor of anarchy. Even though I periodically break these rules, often with gusto, they still apply to the vast majority of my purchases, so my overall budget can tolerate the exceptions. These rules are crucial to running a stress-free store; they create a win-win situation in which I have nothing to lose and lots to gain. Low risk, high return, and all that jazz.

## LOVE AT FIRST MATH

Sometimes the main reason I fall in love with a new source is simply math. I've got a mercurial history of feelings about math, but when it's love, it's love. Let me tell you one such love story. The first time I set foot inside my now-favorite thrift store (which shall remain nameless in order to spare the feelings of all the others), I'm not gonna lie, I was pretty excited by the slightly chaotic, disheveled, dusty vibes. You read right—those were promising qualities in my eyes. In my experience, these are some of the most common conditions for treasure-hunting fortune. There was also a *lot* of stuff. I settled in for a thorough, methodical comb-through of the whole store.

I was making my way around the big metal shelves full of all manner of housewares spanning about a century of interior design styles, when I saw the back wall covered in similar shelves, but full of shoes. As is the case in many high-volume, donation-based charity shops and thrift stores, there was a sign indicating item prices for the whole section rather than pricing on each individual item. Great, I thought, that's also a good figurative sign. They want to move these shoes! The literal sign indicated that the shoes cost three dollars a pair; I was already jumping for joy, because that's about half the price of shoes at the nearest Goodwill. But then I noticed the sign also included a *Bulk Price*: 6 pairs of shoes for *six dollars*. That math rocked my world.

It was love at first sight. Well, maybe second sight, because I distinctly remember doing a double take. These shoes were effectively a dollar a pair. I had never, in the history of my store, bought shoes that cheap from any brick-and-mortar establishment. Sure, I had snagged *a* pair of shoes for a buck at the odd yardsale—and felt like I'd struck gold—but this? Unheard of! I could get six pairs of shoes here for the price of one pair at Goodwill, and for the record, the shoes covered a range of quality that was definitely comparable to Goodwill. I'm pretty sure I bought twelve pairs of shoes that day. I know there's a head-over-heels joke in here somewhere, but I'll let you handle that.

I had a recent revelation that I love the store mentioned in this story so much because it's like being at a yardsale—a big, continuous yardsale that always has good stuff, is always open, never gets rained out, and always has yardsale prices! To this day, almost every time I go there, I come home with shoes. Which is good, because shoes sell regularly for good prices. It's so efficient, because if I'm trying to list a large batch of items this month (say, 500), I want the cost of those items to be as low as possible, and their quality to be as high as possible. It's not necessarily that I'm too cheap for Goodwill these days, it's just that I'm strategic. The rest of the items at this shop also have been consistently fresh, good quality, and low-priced, so you can bet that this shop is always going to be a higher-priority source to visit than most others. Plus, this shop directly supports a cause I care about that contributes to the well being of my fellow humans, so I'm doubly happy to support their business as much as possible.

# A Note About Thrift Stores

Some people I've encountered feel guilty about buying things from a thrift store because of their perception that low-cost items should remain available exclusively for people who can't afford to pay more for things for their own personal use. I understand that point, but thanks to my time and experience in the secondhand realm, I also understand that most successful thrift stores are all about moving volume—in other words, they want to sell a lot of stuff quickly and consistently. If I can be one of their best customers (making regular large-ish purchases), I'm helping to invest in the business of the thrift store itself, and in turn, the causes they support, as well as helping to ensure that they will be able to continue funding their causes for years to come. I learned a lot about this (and so much more—wow!) in the book *Secondhand* by Adam Minter, which I highly recommend. Also —and I really can't stress this enough—there is just *So. Much. Stuff!*

Most people never bring it up, but occasionally a cashier will ask what I'm doing with all this stuff. I often tell them I love thrift shopping, I am a regular thrift-store customer, and I also resell some of the items I buy, and it's true! I shop for my store regularly, but I also love to buy items for certain friends and family of mine who love certain things—like the occasional Batman for John, gently used baby clothes for my niece, vintage silk shirts for myself, and bolts of fabric and fancy trims for my friend Amanda, who is a historical costume designer. My eBay store (and the necessary sourcing of items) really is a natural extension of the way I personally shop: with nostalgia, special favorites of myself and my loved ones, and the right price point in mind. In short, if you want a local thrift store to consistently provide low-cost items to your community, donate to it and shop it regularly. Both are necessary to keep that thrift store thriving.

ANNA PACKER

# THE SHOP

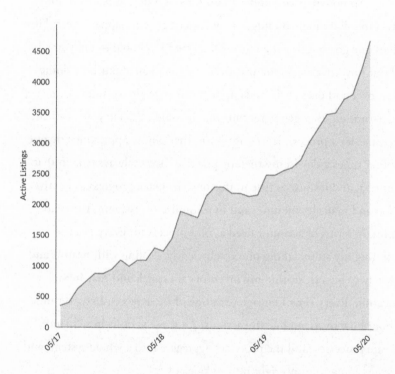

*How does it work?*

# CHAPTER 4: HELLO, SYSTEMS

So now that you know about tons of different places to find stuff to sell online, you might be wondering what happens next. How does one go about selling said stuff online? I'm going to tell you all about how that works for any given item, and all about how doing that over and over again adds up to a full time gig (or in my case, a part-time gig that generates full-time income). Buckle your seatbelt, because it's a process. Ironically, I said that phrase approximately one zillion times a day in my therapy practice. It was always true in that context, and it's just as true in this one. To make progress as I actively plan and manage my time, and to minimize overwhelm, I *have* to think in terms of action. I need a solid process for every facet of running my store: taking photos efficiently, dealing with returns and crotchety buyers, storing my inventory for quick and easy item location. Every time I engage with one of these facets, I try to think about how to streamline my actions. All those actions in sequence create processes, and the processes aggregate into a whole system, and we are going to jump right into its nucleus.

## THE GARAGE

If you've been paying attention, you already know that each of my items has a virtual home on eBay, but my main storage space for inventory is my (formerly) two-car garage. It started with a couple of shelves, and has grown into a (very organized) monster. I mean, who knew a 4,000-item store could fit into the better part of a two-car garage? This arrangement has worked well for me, though I am just now getting to the point of considering auxiliary storage options. I don't know if that will mean a storage unit, paring down even more of our personal belongings which currently take up the remaining part of the garage, or something else altogether.

The best thing about keeping my inventory in the garage is that it's not in my living space, and it's still extremely convenient because I don't have to leave my house to access it! That is very important to my mental health and well being. It's certainly nothing fancy, but I have everything I need out there: my shipping station (with my trusty envelope sorter); lots of shelves and bins to organize, store, and protect my inventory; a step stool; and some extra lighting.

## A Day in the Life

While I do love spending time in my garage working on my eBay store stuff, hanging out in the garage is not actually the main draw for running this business, if you can believe that. Of course I do a fair amount of work to run the store, but I have always done a fair amount of work in every job and every business I've ever run. For me, flexibility, freedom of choice, and an ideal work environment make all the difference. I'm going to walk you through a typical weekday in my life to show you just what I mean. I don't generally engage in every process within the overall eBay store system I use every single day, and there are many days in which I don't work on eBay at all, or I only ship things out (like today: I'm sitting on my back porch writing this book). This example is simply meant to paint a picture for you of a standard-ish day in the life of my eBay store:

Today I woke up, started the coffee and slopped the hogs (i.e. fed Cinder and Dobby), and then fixed my coffee and joined John at the kitchen table. John and I love to hang out together in the morning, just waking up and chatting about the day ahead over some delicious, piping-hot coffee. After a half hour or so, John adjourned our coffee hour to get ready for work, and I got down to business logging about 60 items I'd collected from three sources earlier this week: my house, a local non-profit thrift store, and eBay itself. I added each item to my master inventory spreadsheet, researched each item as needed, priced each item, and logged other relevant information, like how much I paid for it and where it came from. This kind of data entry might seem tedious, but today I enjoyed logging with a grisly episode or two of Forensic Files playing in the background.

Once I logged all 60 items, I checked my inventory number; it was about three listings shy of a nice, shiny, clean round number. Because I am a little neurotic and because I can, for my own personal satisfaction, I listed three items I already had waiting for me in the Drafts section of my Listings on eBay. I just love round numbers, don't you?

I then took a morning break, did some housework, wrote a little bit of chapter two of this book, and ate some lunch (including a whole avocado—yum!).

Back to work. This time, I moved the items I had just logged to the area in my garage that serves as a holding zone, where they will wait to be photographed.

After taking photos of each item, I make my way through subsequent stages. I will create listing drafts for them via the eBay app on my phone, then officially list them by completing and publishing the drafts on my laptop, after which I will file the physical items away (back into my garage and into my inventory they shall go) and then someday in the not-so-distant future, I'll pull them out, pack them up, and ship them on to their final destinations. Today, however, I didn't complete the entire lifecycle for these items. I did what seemed most urgent, knowing that every step along the way for each item is pushing the ball forward.

Looking back over my workday (roughly five hours so far), I was very pleased to get these 60 items into the holding zone. My next task was to continue listing for a few hours (I still had about 70 drafts waiting to be listed—I wound up getting through about 25 of them) before it was time to take another break, work on a new song I'm writing, and figure out dinner. By the time John got home, I had logged about 60 items and listed about 28. Even as I write that, I have a couple of different reactions. The first is "Yeesh, that's not very much," and the second is, "Awesome! That was a pretty leisurely day!" Both are correct; typically, the time it takes to log items is unpredictable (mostly because research time varies a lot), but when I list or photograph items, I reliably process 10-20 items per hour, depending on the complexity of the listings.

There have been many days during which I have photographed, drafted, and listed 50+ items, completing the whole cycle start to finish—sometimes as many as 100 (that was probably a

12-hour day)! Today, I'm glad I logged those 60 items and listed nearly half as many drafts, but I definitely want to get those other drafts listed ASAP. The sooner they are listed, the sooner they can sell!

Just like I'm working out my thoughts and feelings about today's work in this paragraph, I frequently assess and reprioritize tomorrow's work based on what happened today. Perhaps I was planning to go out on a big sourcing expedition tomorrow; with this assessment, I might change my plan and stay home, cut out all distractions, buckle down, and list the remaining 40-something items before I introduce any new inventory into the mix. It all depends on what seems to be the most salient way to push the ball forward, to be as effective as possible, and still spend my time in a way that I actually enjoy.

## STAGES

The picture I just painted (and lived) is just a still frame of a whole motion picture; each stage contains micro processes that make this whole thing work, from the time an item crosses the threshold into my home until it crosses the threshold on its way out. I'm going to describe each stage and its inherent micro processes in some detail —quirks, tips, and all!

## STAGE 1: LOGGING

Once a given item is purchased or otherwise procured for my eBay store, it's lifecycle as a piece of inventory truly begins with being logged in my inventory spreadsheet. This very important initial stage contains several micro processes: documenting already-known information, researching as needed for additional information, and ultimately creating the title and setting the price for each item.

I bring items from my car into my house, usually parking them in the living room. More often than not, I log items the same day I shop to avoid confusion; I don't like to put anything in the garage until it's been logged, in case it accidentally becomes intermingled with already-processed items. Also, I *hate* when any eBay items are cluttering my living space for any reason. If I can't log them that day, I'll leave them in my car until I can log them, if the climate permits. I live in the South; I'm not going to leave a hand-carved candle in my car in mid-August, even overnight.

I purposely stack all items to be logged in front of the TV. It's a total buzzkill, loaded with negative reinforcement. (Which means it's designed to increase the behavior of processing items in order to remove the aversive stimulus of my living room being cluttered and my TV being blocked—not to be confused with punishment, which is characterized by the addition of an aversive stimulus in order to decrease a behavior—I knew those psychology degrees would pay off!) Anyway, the items temporarily pile up, my cats come over and sniff everything, and I bust out my laptop. I open my Google drive, select a spreadsheet called—for real—*eBay Empire*, and open the current inventory sheet, which I use to catalog every item in my store.

On this sheet, each new item has a subject number, title, eBay item identification number, category, source, cost of goods, listing price, and month it was logged. The subject number simply tracks the number of items I've listed over all time (for example, today I logged my 5,430th item of all time, which includes all current actively listed items plus all the listings I've ever ended or sold). The data is also sortable with each string of data having a subject number to anchor it: proof that I actually did learn something in my undergrad research methods lab.

The title is exactly what it sounds like—its just a basic description of the item with as many keywords as possible, formulated by a combination of my own observations and item research. It eventually gets polished up and used as the listing title.

I generally research items with a quick search on eBay using the most basic descriptors: brand, color, style, etc. Some people get super into having the most and best keywords, but I'm admittedly not very particular about it. I generally try to maximize the 80 characters allowed for titles, and to fill it up, I just think about what I would type in if I were trying to find that thing; what are the most important characteristics or identifiers? I also look for common denominators in the language of listing titles for similar items. I am not always 100% thorough about this. If you look in my store right now, I guarantee you'll see more than one item title that is sorely underutilized. That's because I'm a human being who is easily bored, and some days, getting listed with a quick and dirty, C+/B- quality title is just how it has to be. Those items still sell. Could they perhaps sell faster if I titled them better? Maybe, but I just don't care that much about it every single time I'm listing. Mostly, I shoot for A's, but as they say, B's get degrees; so, I keep it moving!

Often when I'm researching a new item, I find a listing for an identical one; in that case, I typically copy and paste the title of the identical one into my spreadsheet, then polish and fit it to my specific item. It's usually a lot faster to do it that way, even if it's something as simple as an Old Navy cardigan with a certain print. Someone else has already toiled over the keywords, maximized the characters, and successfully sold an identical item—no need to reinvent that wheel!

Wait, "Already sold?" you ask? That's right! I search for completed listings and sold items—not just what is currently listed. That helps me see how saturated the market is, the range of prices similar items have sold for, how frequently and how recently identical or similar items have sold, and more. It's an invaluable resource, available on the side toolbar of search criteria on the regular ol' eBay search. It's super helpful for anything that's not 100% unique.

Once in a while, I can't find anything close to my item on eBay —in the sold listings or anywhere else! In that case, I usually do a Google search to generally learn more about the item in order to title and price it according to established value, rarity, condition, and all other things germane to value.

Another advantage of researching items as I log them is that I learn so much! I see things in those search results that I later see at a thrift store or yardsale—it really does inform what I buy! I also learn stuff about my own items that comes in really handy—for example, I have learned several times about brands that are carried at the store Anthropologie; for many of these items, I could tell they were really nice quality and condition, but I'd never heard of the brand. Then, when I researched it just using basic descriptors and the brand name, a bunch of similar items came up that had "Anthropologie" in the titles! No wonder they were such cool designs and quality materials— this stuff is from Anthropologie, which also means it generally has above-average resale value. That kind of thing is so good to know!

Every item is also assigned to a category during the logging stage. My categories are not the same as eBay's listing categories in terms of specificity; rather, they are broad and mainly function to help me to know generally where in storage each item is. The categories I assign include: Accessories, Clothing, Craft Supplies, Ephemera, Housewares, Media, Shoes, and Toys & Collectibles. I also log the source—was it from a thrift store? A yardsale? A freebie?—and how much I paid for each item. Over time, this has shown me which sources typically yield the most profitable items, the most items, and the lowest cost of goods; obviously, the free stuff has the lowest cost of goods, but there's no consistent source for free stuff, and not all free stuff is worth listing. It all works together to make the shopping part of the process more efficient; plus, it's so fun to track all this data. I had a blast compiling the list of sources for this book, thanks to my trusty spreadsheets. Over time, I can see trends and ask new, more nuanced questions. I love being able to use this information to source smarter!

I log the cost of goods in part because I love seeing the return on my investment in individual items. I do have an uncanny ability to remember where I bought most items and how much I paid for them, but I'd rather have the data deposited fresh into my spreadsheet to be a reliable witness years from now when I surely won't remember. By the way, I've spoken to numerous other thrifters who possess this remarkable ability to remember exactly what an item cost, years later; I'm not the only one! Could I just keep track of overall sourcing expenses? Sure, but why forego the fun?

Finally, after considering what I already knew or just learned via research on any given item, I set a listing price during the logging stage, which I will confirm and actually enter into the item listing during the listing stage. Unless I'm concerned about it being difficult to break even on an item—which simply does not happen because my cost of goods is so low—the price I paid to acquire an item is the *last* thing I would factor into its listing price. Ever heard that beauty is in the eye of the beholder? I'm putting these items on eBay for the ideal Beholder, not necessarily for people who are looking for the rock-bottom price on something. The Beholder and I are always on the same page, because we both see the actual value of the item. The reason I ended up with this item in the first place is because the thrift store or yardsale or auction was pricing it to move, not to maximize the true value of the item. Don't worry though—I know my pricing isn't perfect. There's a remedy for that, too: a Best Offer.

I'm bringing up the eye of the beholder because I've known other resellers to wring their hands about it. No one has to know I paid 50 cents for something; it's not a secret, it's just none of their business. If I'm not charging something exorbitantly high according to the established *market value* of the item I've discovered by researching the item, then *I don't worry about it.* My customers are paying for the convenience of online shopping; among other things, they are paying for the my eye, intuition, and time, all of which work together to make an item available to them in the first place. They aren't just reimbursing me for the monetary expense I incurred to be able to sell it.

The final data point I log for each item is the current month: the month in which it was logged! I generally try to procure, log, and list items within the same month, so this number serves as an approximate date for when the item was originally obtained and listed. It's really helpful, the longer my store operates, to have this metric. Just last week, I sold something I'd had in my garage for 27 months! It was great to be able to look at the logged information and instantly know how old that item was.

I also thoroughly enjoy looking at a string of item data whenever something sells; it's like a mini case study. I copy and paste the string of item data from the inventory log into a *Sold* page in my spreadsheet, where shipping cost and other data are added to the string, and bam! Suddenly I see the cost of goods juxtaposed with the sale price. Seeing a 50 cent investment sell for 50 bucks is one of the closest things to waving a magic wand that I've experienced, as I'm still waiting on my letter from Hogwarts.

It's worth noting that this whole spreadsheet situation is totally optional, but since it appeals to me (thanks to my aforementioned love of data) and it keeps me organized, I always do this step, no matter what. I'm not interested in a holey data set, know what I mean? There is actually one cell left bank for every item after it's been fully logged in my spreadsheet, though. The one thing that is not entered during the logging process is the eBay item identification number. This is a string of twelve numbers that is assigned to a listing when it goes live, and it's how eBay's internal system tracks the item. I copy and paste this directly from eBay every time a listing goes live, not during logging. You better believe that the eBay identification number column is already set up, ready and waiting by the end of the logging process.

After the formal logging process is over, or sometimes in the midst of it, I will remove all price tags, give things a good look-over and clean them up if necessary. Then, off they go to the holding zone!

## HOLDING ZONE

This is where every item I process gets to rest for a spell after being logged and before being photographed, as well as between being photographed and being filed away with the other already-listed inventory. If I didn't already sort or group like items together while grabbing items out of the pile to log them, I sort or group like items right here in the holding zone after logging them in order to set myself up for success in Stage 2, which is photographing all logged items. Sorting at this point in the process is logical, since it's easier for me to photograph all the coffee mugs in a given batch of items, rather than photographing a coffee mug, followed by a stuffed animal, followed by a trenchcoat, followed by a book, followed by another mug—every type of item has certain staging and angles that are most conducive, so I find that organizing these items beforehand really does maximize my time later, even though it might mean a few extra minutes spent in the holding zone. This also allows me to think about and scope out where these items will ultimately be stored after they are photographed and listed.

The physical space I'm referring to as the loading zone is not exactly a convenient space. My garage, though well-organized, is pretty full, so the only available space is the aisle between the two main rows of steel shelves that hold most of the inventory. It's not ideal, because if I need to maneuver around the holding zone to pull an item for shipping, all the logged-but-not-yet-listed stuff is totally and utterly in my way. However, that does create another nice little current of negative reinforcement, encouraging me to get those items processed quickly, so I can move them out of my way once and for all in the filing stage. Sometimes, it's unavoidable, and I just have to move stuff around. The show must go on!

## STAGE 2: PHOTOGRAPHING

Most of the time, the vast majority of information potential buyers want about an item is in the photos, or *should* be. If pictures are worth a thousand words, eBay gives us all 12,000 words per listing to work with, and it has nothing to do with the item description box. Every listing includes 12 photos to convey everything there is to know about this item. I do still fill out item specifics and a minimal description in the process of listing, but honestly, people don't rely on descriptions as much anymore, especially on eBay's mobile app which is utilized by a *massive* chunk of online shoppers. For the most part, it's all about the photos.

No matter what, it's advisable to maximize the available photo spots by shooting clear, well-lit photos on a neutral background of some kind. Bonus points if I can show measurements in the photos, because yes, people want to know exactly how tall that oversized coffee mug is. I do my best to get as many high quality photos, showing the item in the most comprehensive way that I can manage. However, that doesn't mean I use all 12 photos for every single item. Some things, like vintage brooches for example, might only need four to six quality photos to effectively convey everything you'd ever want to know about them. That's totally fine. Elaborately beaded ball gowns, on the other hand, might be difficult to thoroughly capture with only 12 photos. I just have to do the best I can, case by case. Oh, and for the record, there is no fancy equipment involved; at least, nothing fancier than an iPhone 8. I take all my photos with a phone, and it works like a charm.

One thing I wish I had figured out *years* earlier than I did, was to take photographs with the screen locked and already set in a square shape so they don't have to be rotated or cropped—this literally saved hours of my life, and I don't even want to think about how many hours I wasted before I figured this out. It's gut wrenching, as reality sometimes can be. Another thing about photographing that can't be stressed enough is: *I don't fear showing the flaws!* In fact, I make them super obvious. I always disclose and describe any flaws or issues, and for good measure, in the condition description, I always point people to the pictures to assess the flaws for themselves.

Does a buyer occasionally insist that a manufacturing seam, clearly pictured in the photos, is in fact a crack, leave me a negative review, and ultimately return the item? You bet. Even if I disagree with a buyer's claim, I'm still going to find a way to make it right and always strive to make an honest assessment of the situation. Do I occasionally overlook something and fail to notice or disclose a flaw? Of course. There are bound to be a handful of honest mistakes to be found among four or five thousand listings. Sometimes the mistakes result in returns, which I always accept. Often I can relist the items and adjust the listings to reflect the flaw I had previously overlooked in just a few seconds; occasionally I'll even add an additional photo of the flaw in question. That's just about the only time photographing takes place outside the usual sequence of processing an item. Either way, I'll relist it and most likely sell it again.

I always try to use the best light possible when taking photos, which is usually natural light. I'll even schedule the rest of my to-do list for the day around the best-lit hours in the room where I take photos. I have a light kit, but would rather use natural light any day. With natural light streaming in, (or my cowboy light kit blazing away, for the occasional night time shoot,) Stage 2 is where I binge my favorite podcasts, learn music for upcoming singing engagements, and sometimes even think deeply about the stuff I'm currently creating. I've had lots of new ideas while fluidly working my way through a huge pile of stuff, taking photos.

I like to bring a whole batch of stuff into the room where I photograph it (on a big, flat, king-sized bed), chew through that whole pile, and then take it back to the garage to swap it out for the next batch. I find that this is much more efficient for me: few trips between the bedroom and the garage, and items already at hand for a fast photo session. After it's all said and done, everything has been photographed and put back into the holding zone, where it will wait again to be filed away among like items. That's it for this stage!

## STAGE 3: DRAFTING

If I'm having a fairly high-octane day of processing items, there comes a time a few hours into photographing when my back might start hurting from Photographer's Lean, my phone battery is getting low, and I just need to come up for air. These are perfect opportunities to plug in my phone, recline on a bed or couch, and upload the photos from my phone into a listing drafts via the eBay app. It is possible to take photos directly in the eBay app, which in theory should be even faster, but for reasons that are likely both hardware- and software-related, I find the photos taken through the app less efficient for me. I always end up with the app closing spontaneously, the photos coming out blurry or just corrupted (and then I have to pull the item back out and rephotograph it—super annoying), or the app just running too slowly. It's just one of those particular preferences I have; it might seem counterintuitive, but my way works well (and fast) for me.

Creating drafts is also pretty mindless and allows me to take a bit of a breather in the middle of a high-volume processing day.

To create and add photos to a new listing draft, I go to the Selling tab in the app, click on List an Item, and then type or dictate a basic description of the item into the search bar which leads to selecting the eBay listing category, and then a draft is automatically created and opened. I click the spot to add photos and select them from my phone's photo bank. After the photos have uploaded, I scroll all the way to the bottom of the draft and save it for later. Then I just rinse and repeat until all the photos are uploaded into their corresponding drafts. It's one of the easiest tasks in the whole process, and I just love seeing those drafts stack up!

## STAGE 4: LISTING

This is the stage in which my present self thanks my past self for the thorough research, title creation, and pricing that happened in the logging stage. I take all the spreadsheet information and the photos I've already uploaded, polish the listing title, complete a bunch of check boxes and fill-in-the-blank items specifics, describe the item condition in detail, and perhaps even write a little bit in the description box. I select the shipping services, handling time, and return policy, set the price and a few other parameters, and finally, publish the completed draft, creating a live listing! It's more or less an i-dotting, t-crossing kind of thing.

It's worth noting here that although I do follow a general pattern for most listings, my inventory is so miscellaneous that I never have gotten much into using templates or using the bulk editor feature to complete listings. On rare occasions, it makes sense; for example, when I'm listing a bunch of the same kind of item and all the individual listings will be sold in the same eBay category, with the same shipping parameters, pricing, etc. Those conditions aren't typical for me though, so my general listing process is to take each listing at a time, fill it out completely, submit it, copy and paste the item's freshly assigned eBay identification number into my inventory spreadsheet, and then move on to the next one.

I list *nearly* every item as a Buy It Now type of listing with the option to receive a Best Offer from potential buyers—no auctions. I am a patient seller who has little capital tied up in my inventory and plenty of storage space, so I can afford to wait for someone to either pay the asking price, or to entertain and accept offers I deem reasonable. *The Scavenger Life Podcast* hosts, Jay and Ryanne, refer to this strategy as "List It and Forget It." If I had to pinpoint one singular concept that totally rerouted my life, it's this one. It totally blew my mind to find out that many sellers who had a spare room or garage or storage building of some kind could build a whole life on a large, relatively slow-turnover online store. I think it's absolutely brilliant; I'm still not over it.

I want to talk about shipping for a moment. But wait, shipping in the listing stage? Yep. Therein lies the rub. One of the sort of tricky things about listing on eBay is figuring out in advance the best way to ship something. You have to decide this at the time you list it, so it warrants a mention here. There is a pretty significant eternal discussion among eBay sellers about offering free shipping (by building the shipping cost into the price of the item) versus having the buyer pay for shipping, either flat rate or calculated rate. I'm not going to get into the debate, but there are worthy considerations on both sides. As with most aspects of running an eBay store, personal preference gets the final say. Since this book is about how I run my store, I'll tell you why I do it the way I do it.

I almost always have the buyer pay for the shipping; in this Amazon world, that might sound absurd, but I refuse to budge on this for one simple reason: *shipping stuff costs money!* Someone will take this casserole dish from north Georgia to Southern California for me, for just *20 bucks?* Are you kidding me? That's a great value!

To me, using calculated shipping (or flat rate, when it makes sense) feels more transparent than building the cost of shipping into the item price. I'm not saying anyone who offers free shipping isn't honest, I just personally feel it's more clear to the buyer and to me when the shipping is explicitly stated, especially in light of how we seem to be collectively forgetting as a society that *shipping stuff costs money!* Plus, it's simpler and more streamlined for me in the listing process; it would take me so much longer if I had to figure in all the potential shipping costs to every item. I'm not against other people building in shipping, but I am perfectly happy overtly charging for it. No free shipping, no free returns (because, again, shipping stuff isn't free), but I do accept returns for all items, for any reason, domestically and internationally. My store is big enough to absorb the occasional refund-and-relist situation, and this helps keep me motivated to do my best on the front end while photographing and listing items.

So, what I need to estimate when I'm listing an item in order to approximate the correct calculated shipping rate is the size of the package the item will be shipped in and the approximate weight. Honestly, at this point I make an educated guess (educated by shipping a couple thousand items over the last three years, that is). This doesn't have to be perfect, but it needs to come close. One of the great things about having estimated package information on the front end is that it makes the shipping process itself really easy once the item sells. For now though, I estimate the size and weight and choose the appropriate shipping service. The vast majority of my items ship USPS First Class or USPS Priority Mail. If it will fit in a USPS Priority Mail padded envelope, great! Then it's flat rate, and anyone can pick up those envelopes for free at the post office, or even better, I order them on USPS.com and have them delivered right to my house! There is admittedly a little learning curve here for new sellers, getting the hang of which shipping services make the most sense for which items, but experience is a great teacher and for me, determining shipping became second-nature pretty quickly. Do I sometimes overestimate or underestimate? Sure I do! It can be a little bit of a hassle, but I don't mind having a bit of room to improve.

I definitely follow the "List It and Forget It" hallmark of *The Scavenger Life* founders' strategy. I like to list my items and leave them alone. Instead of spending my time on tweaking listings or altering prices or updating prices according to market research, I have time to do other (more interesting) experiments, get to know new items, try out new sourcing places, and generally innovate rather than calibrate. My newer listings are probably better quality and more efficient than my older ones, but rather than fuss with changing the older ones, I just keep listing more and always try to do a better job than I did yesterday. This approach promotes overall efficiency for me, because my goal is to get bigger and better, not just one or the other. Besides, Best Offer covers a multitude of sins.

## STAGE 5: FILING

I usually wait until a batch of items is listed to move them from the holding zone into the categorized spaces those items will occupy long-term in inventory. I like to think of this like I'm filing documents; find the correct folder (or drawer, or shelf, or bin, or bag) and tuck each item in with its comrades. I don't have a sophisticated inventory system; I really don't have much beyond labels on bins and generally like items in the same areas. For example, there is one full five-tier steel shelf full of bins, boxes, and bags of stuffed animals, with throw pillows stacked on the top shelf. If a stuffed animal just got listed, I open bins until I see an open space for it, and file it away.

This filing process has a fringe benefit: it keeps my eyes on all the previously filed inventory on a fairly regular basis. I can't tell you how many times something has sold, and I know right where to find it because I recently filed something new into its bin. The only problem here is that I'm the only person on earth who really knows where everything is, and on extremely rare occasions, even I can't find something. I don't think anything has been lost forever, but I spent a couple hours trying to find one very small clothing item once. It was in the completely wrong bin, and I still have no idea how it got there. It might have hitched a ride on some other clothing while I was filing. Who knows! Once an item is filed, it lies dormant in its temporary home while its listing is out working magic on the Internet.

## STAGE 6: SELLING

Fortunately, selling doesn't require anything else on my end! One of my favorite experiences in the world of eBay is selling stuff in my sleep—that should tell you how much selling has to do with my actions at the moment of sale. Of course, I've tried to set every item up for success, so usually people just Buy It Now and I simply get the notification. Sometimes though, I get to choose whether I make a sale, because almost all of my listings include the option for buyers to Make an Offer. I love getting those offer notifications, too! John likes to call these moments of decision "offertunities." You decide who is the cheesier one in the family. It's a close race at this point.

Deciding whether to accept an offer or counteroffer (or sending an offer to watchers, a new-ish feature on eBay) is definitely the most direct way I influence a sale, but aside from actually listing the items, there are a few other things in my control that certainly contribute to sales. I often run promotions; a favorite of mine is $5 off anything $19.99 or more. While I don't offer free shipping, I will frequently accept offers that basically account for the shipping cost if it's generally a reasonable offer. Also, I list pretty regularly. I don't think there is necessarily any back-end algorithm magic that comes from listing regularly, but there is some small percentage of all items that sell quickly, so the more I list, the sooner and more consistently all those quick-sellers will sell.

Even less direct, I do spend some amount of time answering potential-buyer messages with questions about items, although there are many times I don't answer these at all if I don't have time that day. I accept returns for any reason, so if someone wants to try something out and I haven't answered their incredibly nit-picky question, they aren't going to be stuck with that item if it doesn't work out. The truth is, if my listing isn't comprehensive enough already for a certain buyer (let's say for example, someone who wants me to measure the thickness of the decorative trim of a jacket, or to tell them "how blue it is") the I'd probably rather just wait for another buyer.

One more way I spend my time in the area of selling is by making my favorite moves within my trusty spreadsheet. For each item that has sold, I go to the page that contains the initial item listing information, search the eBay-given item ID number (or title, if needed), highlight the item title in bright green (for *Cash Money*), and copy and paste that item's data string onto the *Sold* page of my spreadsheet. It's a sweet, sweet copy-paste!

## STAGE 7: SHIPPING

Welcome to the final stage! *This* step is one of the most fun, in my opinion, probably second only to shopping. I always joke that it's got something to do with my last name. They don't call me Packer for nothing, har har. I'll definitely keep saying it; you can't stop me. (I think I just took the lead in the "Cheesiest" competition.) In any case, once I locate an item in inventory storage, I pull it for shipping, which just means I take it from its storage spot and pile it with the other items going out on a big folding table that serves as my shipping station in the garage. I have consistently shipped things out two or three times per week for the last three years, with my handling time typically set at three business days, but lately I've been experimenting with one business day, and at least anecdotally, it seems to have increased sales a little bit. It's hard to say with certainty how much decreasing my handling time helps sales, since there are so many other factors in play at any given time. For now, I don't mind shipping every other day or even daily, so if it seems to be helping a little bit, it can't hurt.

Gathering and packing everything at the same time, whether it's every other day or every three or four days, is an important pillar of efficiency in my system. I like to do everything in batches, so that I can maximize my efforts and ideally be in action long enough to experience flow in each task. Shipping is no exception.

Now, I am a scrappy shipper, so I've got all kinds of recycled shipping materials (thank you, Amazon) as well as eBay-branded shipping materials which are available to eBay store subscribers once a quarter (for free, up to a certain amount, but I can buy more anytime), plus a couple of key tools that make shipping a pure joy: a small scale (thanks, Mom!), a heavy-duty tape gun, a measuring tape, and a *gorgeous* Dymo thermal label printer (my pride and joy).

I pack each item, confirm the actual weight, dimensions, and shipping service selection, and print my postage label right from eBay, which not only gives me a discount on the postage, but also allows me to seamlessly pay for shipping and have tracking automatically uploaded, plus it automatically notifies the buyer that their item has shipped. I almost always ship via USPS, occasionally using a FedEx or UPS service for heavy or bulky items, like furniture. Not only is USPS almost always the cheapest and fastest choice, but I utilize a handful of other services and products offered by USPS, all of which are totally free available to anyone!

Discovering the USPS free shipping supplies and services really upped my shipping game. One of those beloved freebies from the post office, I've already mentioned: free priority mail shipping supplies. I use the heck out of their Priority Mail Flat Rate Envelopes. Another freebie is really just about borrowing. I tend to borrow several corrugated plastic mail bins—all you have to do is ask at the counter—and voila, my postal carrier's life is so much easier! I put all my securely packaged items into one (or two or three) of those bins, and then, there's only one thing left to do: utilize the best USPS free service of them all.

## SCHEDULING A PICKUP

Technically, this is still part of shipping, but I'm giving pickups their own section because they really are miraculous. I didn't know scheduling a pickup was an option for the longest time; no regrets, but seriously—I took so many unnecessary trips to the post office! If shipping is the final stage, scheduling a pickup is the victory lap. Plus, it still feels like magic to me, even though I have been scheduling pickups for well over a year. Anyone with a free USPS.com account and an eligible mailing address can do this. If your carriers drop off your mail at your home, there's a good chance they can pick most things up from the same location for free on their regular postal route!

All I have to do is go to the USPS website, log in, and there is a little form to fill out (called "Schedule a Pickup," of course) that confirms my address, where my items will be (on the porch, in the mailbox, etc.) and asks approximately how many packages of each mail class are included in the pickup (e.g. 6 Priority Mail, 3 First Class) and the approximate combined weight. I then can select the date and time of pickup (during regular mail delivery is free) and submit the form. Then I sleep like a baby, shove my corrugated plastic bin of packages onto the front porch as the coffee is brewing the next morning, and the mail carrier faithfully picks it up right from my front porch. Sometimes, she even leaves me a replacement bin. It's the best.

So, that's the whole system that encompasses the lifecycle of every item in my store. Easy peasy, right? Sure, the system takes time and requires hard work, but it works well for me. I like to work in batches and think in stages for many reasons; one of the top reasons is that it helps me build an experiential knowledge base to draw from when I'm trying to plan out my afternoon or week or month. I can roughly estimate, with a decent degree of accuracy, how long the upcoming stages will take to complete. That actually helps me spend less time hemming and hawing about what to do and when to do it, and most importantly, it helps me free up the most possible time for *all the other good stuff in life*. After all, that's why I started running this store in the first place.

## OTHER ASSORTED TASKS

Being able to estimate my time investment into the eBay store for the week is great, but I have to confess, the stages I just walked you through don't account for every single solitary thing. There are other assorted tasks that have to be done at some point, and it's much harder to estimate the time it takes to do those kinds of things. This extra time spent can really feel like growing pains. Here are some of the other things you might find me doing in service of my store, with indeterminate frequency and duration:

- Researching individual items I'm considering buying
- Packing bins for my contractor, Watson (I'll introduce him properly a bit later, I promise)
- Reorganizing, streamlining, or upgrading storage components in the garage, such as buying and assembling a new steel shelf, or

dividing a category into sub-categories with their own sections or bins

- Ordering and organizing shipping supplies
- Paying my eBay invoices
- Keeping my spreadsheets in tip-top shape

One could argue that doing these things ultimately saves time, but when I'm trying to figure out how much time to spend on one of those extra activities, it sometimes feels like a big, annoying detour. Typically, I have also waited to do stuff like dividing larger categories into smaller ones until it's become abundantly clear and borderline dire. I have to say that I honestly don't build in time for that stuff; I usually just do it and then analyze how long it took me later, at least to try to learn from the experience and, I hope, get more accurate with estimating the time commitment the next time and actually see the need sooner.

Sometimes I will throw a time-management challenge at myself if I feel like it's something I need to do, but don't really have the time allotted—I'll blitz. I'll give myself a short window, maybe 20-30 minutes, and just try to get the whole thing done in that time (using Parkinson's law to my advantage!) Sometimes, I surprise myself and actually get it done; often I've overestimated how long it would take in the first place, in my initial dread of taking such a detour.

Mostly, I shoot for the moon and land among the stars, and then have a far better idea of how long it will take me to finish what I started. Both those scenarios push the ball forward and feel pretty relieving! A couple of times, I've blitzed into something only to realize it's actually a far-more demanding or tedious task than I originally estimated, or jumping in makes me realize there is some other, larger, more fundamental system that needs to be fixed or totally scrapped, like getting halfway through organizing clothes by size, and then realizing it would be easier to find clothing items if they were grouped by type instead.

It's also worth noting that there are plenty of ways I have not (yet) optimized my store. I don't know a whole lot about what affects ranking and visibility, but the juice of finding out hasn't yet been worth the squeeze for me. The truth is, there's probably no end to how much you can optimize, but realistically you cannot and do not need to conquer every single one (Pareto principle stuff—not to be confused with the burrito principle, in which if it fits in the tortilla, knock yourself out.) For now, I'll keep moving forward, innovating as I go and rarely looking back to calibrate. But who knows? If the juice becomes more compelling, I may very well decide to squeeze after all. Live and learn!

# CHAPTER 5: LEARN & SCALE UP

## PUMP UP THE JAM

Sometimes, when I'm trying to reach a higher overall baseline of inventory, I have to really crank up the volume: a big push to me is 500+ items in a month. This would easily take me 10-20 hours of shopping time, 5-10 hours of logging, 25-50 hours photographing, 5-10 hours drafting, 25-50 hours listing. If you're counting, that's at the very least 70 hours, probably more likely somewhere between 70 and 140, and possibly more! That's also not including the time it takes to pull, pack, and ship whatever sells during the month—all of which vary greatly. I hope you're starting to get the picture—that this is not easy, quick income per se. I can easily work 40 hours a week just like anybody at a traditional 9-5 if I am so inclined.

When I'm going for a big push, I typically still work in batches, even though that means each stage will take much longer than usual. I shop once a week or so, log until it's all logged, then photograph for at least a day or two solid, create the drafts between photography sessions whenever my phone needs to charge, and then list for several full days, all the while shipping stuff out like normal, a couple of times a week. And let's not forget the aforementioned quick-sellers! It's common that the same day I list a bunch of stuff, some of the things I just listed will sell. Maybe one or two, or even more sell the week following that batch of listings, and so on. There are always a few items that sell quickly, which is a great motivation to list when sales feel slow.

## THE ACTUAL COST OF DOING BUSINESS

While I try hard to keep my cost of goods really low, there are definitely other costs associated with running my eBay store; the kicker is, many of these are necessary fixed expenses over which I have little to no control. Some of them I have to pay upfront, but most are sale-dependent:

For example, I currently pay a monthly fee for an Anchor Store subscription, which includes 10,000 fixed price listings. It's $349.99 up front each month to keep all of my listings active regardless of whether a single one of my items sells. That amount may sound like a lot, but not really when you compare it to the $1200 per month I'd be paying for the same number of individual listings if I didn't have a store subscription. (Store subscription = discounted listing fees and other perks.)

Then, there are the sale-dependent expenses, such as final value fees (charged by eBay) on the sale price and shipping costs which are incurred as soon as the buyer pays for their purchase (eBay has specific, category-dependent percentages which are slightly cheaper for store subscribers than for the casual eBay seller without an official store). There are also transaction processing fees associated with buyers' payments charged by PayPal, the recent addition of internet sales tax collected by eBay, and of course, the shipping cost itself. Typical example: a black wide-brimmed wool hat.

| Purchase Price | eBay Final Value Fee | PayPal Fee | Sales Tax | Shipping Cost | Profit |
|---|---|---|---|---|---|
| $26.81 | $2.29 | $1.08 | $1.81 | $6.94 | $14.69 |

There are also shipping overages I occasionally have to eat and partial refunds I occasionally disperse to make a transaction right if something goes wrong. Then, there is the cost associated with purchasing more items for inventory and all the somewhat-less necessary but worthy expenses like storage bins and shelves, labels, tape, and other materials and tools.

Let's just say it's a lot to track; not overwhelming in my experience, but there are details aplenty. I am careful to track all the numbers I need to assess my progress, costs for the month, payouts to myself for my actual income, and a monthly roundup of all the various fees. This helps me see how much of my gross sales is translating to my actual income, and from there, decide how much I want to reinvest into my store.

Honestly, watching the growth has been thrilling, even though it hasn't been rapid. I love how tangible it is, and how measurable a lot of it can be. That being said, I only obsessively crunch and devour numbers when I'm enjoying it. I don't sit and stress about my numbers; when I'm getting antsy, I find some more stuff to list and get to work. When I'm feeling good, I look at the numbers for fun. Numbers are my friends, and I want to keep it that way. Regardless of my feelings, I build in all this data input into certain points in the process, and I assess at the end of every month.

Beyond the monetary expenses, there are other kinds of costs. Precious real estate in the garage and opportunity cost concerning the other items I might have sourced if my queue (and inventory budget) hadn't been already spoken for, and lots of opportunity-cost in terms of profit potential anytime I accept a Best Offer. Maybe most importantly though, there is the personal cost of doing this work. Come with me on a quick detour, and I'll explain.

## THE OTHER COSTS OF DOING BUSINESS

I am the most important part of my business. Before you decide I'm a narcissist, hear me out, because if you run a one-person operation of any kind, you're the most important part of your own operation, too. For my eBay business, I'm it. I make all the decisions. I determine and do or oversee all the work. I assume the risks. I take the responsibility. I provide the customer service. I enact all the changes. I'm the heart. And before all of those things, I'm a person who needed a big change in her life, especially in her work life. Yes, we are wired for work as human beings, and yes, I have already insisted that I love work! But all work costs us personally; we pour out our precious resources of time and energy, commitment and passion, our mental bandwidth, emotions, and creative juices in order to accomplish any and every kind of work.

So what does this work cost me, the person who set out in need of rest, restoration, and space? Running my eBay business costs me far less, especially emotionally, than my therapy practice. At the same time, it costs me a good bit more than just one very full two-car garage. I'll tell you right now, both cars are in the driveway for the foreseeable future. But also, where do I keep my mind, heart, and identity as I embrace a lot of solitude to do this sometimes-lonely work? Where do I keep myself in all this? What if the cost becomes too great? To sustain the heart of my business, I find it imperative to ask myself these questions, and answer them honestly, on a regular basis.

We're rounding the corner on our personal detour here, but I want to take one more moment of your time to acknowledge that most of the eBay store operations chug along with very little necessary interaction with other people. I am fond of saying "there are no emergencies on eBay," which was not the case in my previous line of work, and that's largely because eBay is a way-less-directly interpersonal business. But of course, when one of the hats an eBay seller must wear is for the head of customer service, you can bet that sometimes there is going to be trouble. And trouble costs us all, in the form of money, time, and stress. So what about when other eBay users are abrasive or downright angry toward me? It's easy to be anonymously nasty on the Internet, but I want to grow and be *more* myself and act even *more* consistently with my character and values. All of that is well and good until the first return case shows up on the doorstep.

## RETURN OF THE JUMPER

Nearly five blissful months had gone by—I had made over two thousand dollars in my fledgling store of about 875 items—when my first return happened in September of 2017. It was a doozy: a dreaded INAD (item not as described) case. This one really tested me; I daresay I've never since had a return as dramatic as this one! The Saddlebred corduroy jumper. I was thrilled to buy this item for 25 cents and sell it for over $30, and it might have been the only thing I sold that week—so the return almost made me wish I'd never found it in the first place.

This buyer was *angry*, clearly, for some reason, this overall-style jumper dress didn't fit her the way she thought it would, and she was keen to take out her rage on me. It was really upsetting, because I listed this thing to the best of my ability, in good faith, and she barraged me with messages. It honestly just made me feel bad! And defensive! I was well versed in taming big, dysregulated emotions in charged-up therapy sessions, but these little pings in my eBay inbox were genuinely getting to me. At the end of the day, I of course accepted the return (that was never in question), and I wound up reselling the item later for a higher price to a supremely satisfied buyer (not gonna lie, that felt good).

I did manage to learn a couple of important lessons when it was all said and done: keep calm and provide measurements upfront as clearly as possible. Even though I thought my photos were really good, I had included "measurements by request" in the item description only, thinking that surely the sizing indicated on the inside tag of the item would suffice. Spoiler alert: it does not suffice. Now, I provide measurements in the photos of every clothing item and most non-clothing items. Again, numbers are my friends, and tape measures don't lie or give opinions.

Perhaps an even more important lesson bestowed upon me by this awful return experience is about what taking responsibility is, and what it is not. Taking responsibility is about making the buyer whole by accepting a return and issuing a refund as soon as the item arrives back on my doorstep intact. It is about unconditionally prompt, respectful, and clear communication. Taking responsibility is not about accepting abuse from an angry person, grovelling, or defending myself as a person of integrity. Taking responsibility is enough; everything else is noise.

In hindsight, that first-ever return case seems like it was a test, and I think I passed. I learned, adjusted my process, and moved on. These days, my store is robust enough to absorb any momentary concern about refunds or the mildly irritating process of accepting a return, and it's my joy as a store owner to provide good customer service and make things right if they happen to go off the rails. My store has the sheer mass to soften the blows, but it's also provided me with lots and lots more experience than what I had when that first return came in. That makes all the difference. I don't sweat it anymore. I am far better equipped now to take the occasional trouble as it comes and rest in knowing that the best thing I can do, every time, is the right thing.

Another thing that starting and growing this store has cost me is pride. There's a fun little nuance to figuring out what you're doing, which goes a little like this: you finally feel like you have it together, you get a little confident spring in your step, and then you totally, irreparably mess up—and you know you should have known better. Does it sound like I'm speaking from experience? I am.

## CLAIMING INSURANCE

I was meeting my friend Sarah (hey, Sae Sae!) for coffee the day I got a message from a buyer and my heart dropped right into my stomach. I couldn't stop thinking about it, and even told Sarah about it while we sipped our coffees. The buyer had said that sadly, this beautiful little porcelain cat I had sold had arrived smashed into many, many pieces. There were pictures. It was gnarly. The buyer was very sad, and asked for a refund. I was so bummed the cat had broken, and I was embarrassed! I'm a Packer, after all! How could I have packed it so poorly? I refunded her immediately, and fortunately was able to file a claim with the post office, since the box was also rather smashed. The buyer was very kind about it, but I'll never forget what she said at the end of our exchange: Thank you for refunding me and making this quick and easy . . . but I'd still rather have had the cat.

Oof. Me too, friend. Me too. I think about that cat every time I pack something fragile now, not out of self-punishment or shame, but in the spirit of remembering it's okay to be wrong and to mess up, and out of my commitment to do better next time—every next time.

As I mentioned, relative to my therapy practice, eBay costs me virtually nothing, emotionally. It's nearly always true. As demonstrated in the previous story, that hasn't been the case at every single moment, and even now, people message me to scold me for pricing too high, to ask a million tedious questions only to not buy, to insist they could buy an identical item from another seller for a fraction of the price (be my guest), or to afflict me with a hundred other small annoyances. I think most of these occur because of the relative anonymity we enjoy on such a huge online platform as eBay, hiding behind usernames and avatars.

However, sometimes I get to have great interactions with my basically anonymous fellow humans, like one guy who messaged me to gently correct me, out of the goodness of his heart, about a vintage ball cap I had listed as Michigan Wolverines instead of the Wisconsin Badgers. I know, I know, I'm so sorry—it was a really old and weird version of the logo—please send me your hate mail. Numerous people have circled back to shoot me a message saying thanks and telling me how perfect their item was on arrival. That stuff warms my heart. Nowadays, the good far outweighs the bad, and most of my interactions with buyers wind up making my day.

## SOLVABLE

One of the best things this work affords me is a different kind of creativity. Therapy built my creative muscles in certain ways; writing and performing and consuming music builds them in other ways. Running this store is a whole different animal! I wanted to mention this as a cost of doing business because this kind of problem solving (that makes me feel like MacGyver sometimes) does cost time, unconventional thinking, and perseverance. It's a whole lot of starting where you are, using what you have—and that's before you even get to the real problem solving.

Where the heck is this batch of 200 new items going to go? How is it going to integrate into my storage? Does it mean reorganizing some tubs? Enlisting a friend to help re-fold 300 shirts to maximize space (thanks, Tina!)? Zip tie a crate to the end of the shelving unit? I don't know, but I trust that it's solvable. That's creativity, and creativity is empowering.

ANNA PACKER

# THE INVENTORY

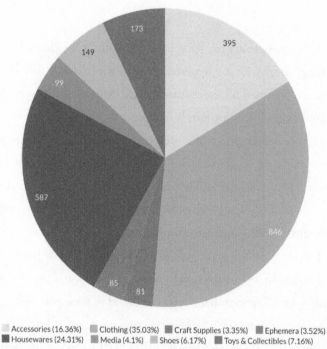

Accessories (16.36%)  Clothing (35.03%)  Craft Supplies (3.35%)  Ephemera (3.52%)
Housewares (24.31%)  Media (4.1%)  Shoes (6.17%)  Toys & Collectibles (7.16%)

*What kinds of stuff do you sell?*

## CHAPTER 6: TANGIBLES

### MISCELLANY

When people ask me what I sell, I usually reply, "literally everything." Bear with my hyperbole, because it certainly feels that way. Hence, I named my store Annaesthetic Miscellany. I'd seen other cute shop names including words like "decor," "fashion," and "vintage," but somehow, I knew even from the beginning that none of those words was inclusive enough. How could my name account for mid-century brass mallard bookends and Trotters woven leather loafers and graduate-level textbooks and framed artwork and stuffed animals and brooches and music boxes and curtains and you get my point. I didn't want to pigeonhole myself into one narrow lane.

I realize that's not the best in terms of branding. One reason I love selling on eBay so much is that the brand of your personal store doesn't necessarily have a lot of bearing on your sales, at least not for me and my store. If I've had repeat customers, I haven't really noticed, to be honest. I sell a little of everything to a little of everyone, all over the world. So, maybe the name ultimately doesn't matter. Still, I wanted my name to feel like a good fit—at least in spirit, representative of the stuff in the shop. The *miscellany* in the shop.

Before I dive in deep to the nature of my particular miscellany, I need to make one proclamation: there's plenty of stuff to go around. There's room for everyone. For real. I mean it. I'll say it a hundred times. When I start telling people about my store, even just mentioning it, they are fascinated and they ask loads of questions, which is fun. Interestingly, these conversations occasionally lead to someone giving me their old stuff, perhaps even consigning more valuable pieces, and referring me to other great inventory sources! They remember that I have this pretty legit eBay store, and the next time there's a stuff-related transition happening in their world, I come to mind! This is a great fringe benefit of being open (abundance) rather than secretive and competitive (scarcity).

I've had friends and family who were decluttering (thank you, Mari Kondo) or downsizing or moving, and they enlisted me to help them get stuff out of their house. They got peace of mind, the hot commodity of space, and free pickup of the stuff they are getting rid of at their convenience. I, in return, got free inventory to sell in my store. It's awesome, once in a blue moon when it happens.

And you know what? If they wanted to start their own store rather than giving me their stuff, I'd cheer them on and hand them my brain for picking! I'd share some of my free shipping supplies with them to help them get started; I'd even write a book about it! I'm not worried about being overrun by competitors, because I firmly believe there's room for all of us who are willing to actually do the work.

Donations aside, the abundance mindset is so important when I'm out doing my regular sourcing. I believe that my mindset has a lot to do with my ability to notice and ultimately bring home quality inventory in the quantities I need to keep going. The stuff is out there, but if I don't believe it's there for me to find any- and everywhere, I'm very likely to overlook it and confirm my fear that there isn't enough stuff. And that does happen, rarely. There are days I go out to find inventory, and every place seems to be a "miss" rather than a "hit." I feel like I've wasted time. Then, I can go to another area, different thrift stores, or change venues entirely and bid online on a local estate sale auction, or otherwise change it up somehow, and end up with a carload of great stuff for 20 bucks.

The longer I do this, the more I learn, and the more value I see in items I would have overlooked before, simply for not knowing enough about them. For example, I was listening to an episode of The Scavenger Life Podcast one day, and the hosts mentioned a silk necktie of a certain high end brand that sells for upwards of a hundred dollars. This made my ears perk up. A necktie for a hundred bucks? Seriously? If you've ever stepped into a thrift store of any kind, you've probably noticed there are enough old neckties around to lay end to end, stretch into outer space, and circle the moon 47 times. Many are silk. So, needless to say, I was thrilled to hear that high-end neckties that sell for over 100 bucks exist in the wild. (I'm not going to tell you the brand name here, because I want you to go listen to *The Scavenger Life Podcast*. It's rad.) I tucked somewhere into my brain the name of the necktie brand mentioned on the podcast, and I kid you not, I found one a couple days later for two dollars at one of my favorite thrift stores. I had never seen one before in my life, at least, not knowingly! Coincidence? I think not. By the way, it sold pretty quickly for over $150.

## THE BIGGER, THE BETTER

It's so fun to get into the details of each individual item, but the predictability and reliability of income is based on the collective impact of the whole inventory. The strategy that serves as the organizing principle of my store is really all about longevity. It's about using time as an asset. The larger the inventory, in theory as well as in my own experience, the more substantial and reliable my income becomes. It all shakes out on a bell curve, and unless some external factors shift around a lot, I can enjoy some relative security in how my store is going to provide for me in the coming months.

This part freaks people out I think, mostly because it's not a guaranteed paycheck every other week for a set amount—it's not even a set hourly wage, although at the end of the week, I do love to calculate my "hourly wage" based on sales that week and the time I clocked working in the store. Just for kicks; data nerd, remember? Just to be clear, I put that in quotation marks because I don't actually pay myself by the hour; I pay myself a conservative, consistent set amount each month, awarding myself with additional bonuses if it's appropriate on an approximately quarterly basis. I find the "hourly wage" simply because I find it to be motivating. I've only been clocking my hours since fall of 2018, so my data is partial on this, but my "hourly wage" since October of 2018, based on hours clocked and net sales in my store, is $18.46 per hour. Not bad for an "unpredictable" part-time gig.

The researcher inside my brain loves this whole side of running an eBay store—which does *not*, by the way, have to be even half as complicated as I've made it. I just enjoy this stuff! Once upon a time, I was enthralled with entering data and running statistical analyses (my thesis partners and I even ran a multinomial logistic regression; say that five times fast), but now I appreciate basic, simple measures of central tendency, variability, and plain old sums more than ever. Sum, Average, Range, and Count are my best friends. I regularly check these sorts of things in my trusty spreadsheets (I don't use any actual equations or internal calculations, by the way—it's just a wall of data I can work with as needed), which helps keep me on track and maintain a big-picture view of my store strategy at work. That also creates a sense of stability.

When I'm enjoying that kind of stability, it's actually fun to take little, measured risks! In terms of buying new things, the worst that can happen is that I break even, or admit my experiment flopped and trash or donate the experimental item. In terms of trying out new sales, promotions, or pricing adjustments in my store, the worst that can happen is that things wind up selling at the normal rate! Smart risks are still risks, but they are always worth taking for the education they provide, if nothing else. The bigger the inventory, the better the experimental environment.

## BREAD, BUTTER, AND CAVIAR

Okay, it's time to immerse ourselves in the actual stuff: the items in my inventory. Hope you're hungry. In each category of items in my store, I've got lots of bread, some butter, and a little bit of caviar. That might sound like a gross sandwich to you, but it's the magical combination that makes my little reselling world go 'round. Let me break it down for you.

## BREAD

Bread includes the most common, bland, and, sorry, but boring items among the inventory. What makes them common, bland, and boring? They are easy to find, have a pretty saturated selling market, are available at low or no cost, and still sell for a decent price—typically $15-30—though they will probably sell slowly. A classic example of Bread is almost any kind of sports team ball cap. I'm sure there are some fancy ones out there, but I'm not talking about the outliers.

I have 20 or 30 listed in my store as I write this. Am I a sports fan, or a ball cap enthusiast? Hardly. Do I sometimes arrive at moments where I never want to touch another snapback again? Sure! But it's a momentary feeling of drudgery. So, I take a break from buying them. The feeling wanes. And once I've recovered from the snapback-doldrums, I buy (and sell) more snapbacks. Go-o-o-o, SPORTS! Hooray, Bread!

## BUTTER

Butter is still commonplace, but slightly more valuable, interesting, and otherwise delicious. (I have been known to eat butter by the spoonful.) These items are still fairly easy to find, but I might pay a little bit more for them, because I know they might sell for $30-$100 or more, rather than under $30. Items analogous to Butter tend to sell more quickly than their Bread peers, partly because their markets are not as saturated (even though they're butter—get it?), partly because they are just tastier. Sorry, not sorry, Bread.

Most of my favorite items are in this category, because a lot of the unique, vintage, and otherwise quirky stuff meets the Butter criteria. One recent example is a super cute vintage Christmas wreath from the 1960s, made totally of beautiful vintage fabrics, featuring a bunch of your favorite characters from the Twelve Days of Christmas. I paid 50 cents for it at a Salvation Army Store this week, listed it the next day, and within an hour it sold for more than 50 dollars. I was delighted the moment I saw it in the store; I loved it, and probably would have paid up to five dollars for it. I was that much more delighted when it immediately sold for a great price—all the hallmarks of Butter!

## CAVIAR

Caviar is, of course, the best, most interesting and expensive of items. The thing about caviar is, even if you want to eat a whole dinner plate full of it, that's not exactly how it works. You won't find it free at your table shortly after your beverage arrives (I'm looking at you, Bread and Butter), and you won't find it in the buffet. If you do, be suspicious (it's probably a knockoff). You have to ask for it, or do the shopping equivalent: look carefully, often and everywhere.

A great example of a Caviar item in my own store was a beautiful vintage sweater. This is a favorite eBay glory story of mine, and probably the one I am wont to tell the most: the Coogi story. This sweater was one of my first few Caviar items; it was a wild, multicolored, one-of-a-kind Australian high end sweater made by Coogi, and popularized by Bill Cosby in the 1980s, and by The Notorious B.I.G. (Biggie Smalls) later on in the 1990s. These sweaters are unmistakable, and truly no two are alike. They are complex tapestries of color and texture, and seriously cool. Here's the story:

John and I are in a tiny, hole-in-the-wall thrift store that supports a homeless ministry, dividing and conquering as usual. John holds up this sweater from a couple of clothing racks away. He says, "Anna, check this out." I do. My jaw hits the floor, because (once again, thanks to *The Scavenger Life Podcast*), I knew exactly what I was looking at. I scrambled over to him to look it over and said, "If this is what I think it is, we are definitely getting it no matter what!" It was in absolutely perfect condition. The tag confirmed it was an authentic Coogi; the red price tag fastener attached by the thrift store confirmed it was two dollars. It took everything in me to finish shopping the rest of the store! We got a few more things, and then rushed home to research and list this Holy Grail of an item. Sure enough, we researched, listed it immediately, and it sold for over $300 to a buyer in Brooklyn, New York in short order.

Caviar items like this one are super exciting to find, but not just because they will transform two bucks into three benjamins. It's exciting because of the exceptional quality, rarity, and cultural value of the item! Those are some pieces of the human experience that connect all of us, and Caviar items tend to be radioactive with specialness, regardless of their potential price point. For the record, I probably would have paid a hundred dollars for that particular Coogi. It happened to cost me only two. Now imagine, if Caviar were overflowing everywhere, how quickly the profits from the sale of the Coogi would compound, if I reinvested them two dollars at a time into more Coogis? Imagine, then tuck away that thought for later.

A couple other factors might affect the food analogy fit of any given item. For example, a Bread item in the right conditions might earn enough bonus points to graduate from Bread to Butter, or something that wouldn't even qualify as Bread might get listed in my store anyway. For example, I have a couple of large lots of vintage postcards and matchbooks. Some are collectible, some sell in lots, some are pretty worthless. Why trifle with them at all? I personally find them to be cool and interesting, they are super cheap or free, and they are quick to get listed, plus very easy to store and ship. On the other hand, if something is super bulky and heavy—a nightmare to store and ship—or is simply incredibly tedious and boring to me, it might get downgraded from Butter to Bread. Caviar, generally speaking, is Caviar.

## Examples of Bread

| CATEGORY | ITEM | COST OF GOODS | SALE PRICE |
|---|---|---|---|
| Clothing | Hot Pink Gap Legging Jean Corduroys Size 26/2r | $1.00 | $27.45 |
| Housewares | Vintage Mebel Italy David Davir Plastic Retro Snack Tray Red Yellow Green Fruit | $0.67 | $27.99 |
| Toys & Collectibles | Disney Parks Stuffed Animal Plush Nala Lion King | $0.15 | $22.99 |

## EXAMPLES OF BUTTER

| CATEGORY | ITEM | COST OF GOODS | SALE PRICE |
|---|---|---|---|
| Clothing | Vintage Light Pink w/White Lace Tosca CA Lingerie Slip Rosebuds Teddy Size L | $0.59 | $56.61 |
| Housewares | Wool Rustic Woven Rabbit Tapestry Pillow Black Velvet Back | $0.50 | $54.39 |
| Toys & Collectibles | Vintage Hard Plush Grey Elephant Trunk Up Black Hard Eyes Pink Ears 10in | $1.01 | $36.59 |

## EXAMPLES OF CAVIAR

| CATEGORY | ITEM | COST OF GOODS | SALE PRICE |
|---|---|---|---|
| Clothing | Vintage COOGI Australia Sweater Size Large Colorful Crewneck Mercerized Cotton 90s Biggie Cosby | $2.00 | $309.74 |
| Housewares | Harris G Strong Water Birds Boat Blue White Gold Framed Mid Century Art Print | $2.00 | $311.04 |
| Toys & Collectibles | Vintage Commonwealth Rare Toy Monkey Knee Hugger Red Overalls & Hat McCrory | $1.01 | $200.39 |

# A Note About Categories

My largest and most diverse categories of items are Clothing, Housewares, and Toys & Collectibles—I felt they would make the best examples. I have several other categories whose examples I didn't include here for the sake of brevity, but you'll see them in some of the charts throughout the book. According to the way I log my items initially, my items categories are as follows: Accessories, Clothing, Craft Supplies, Ephemera, Shoes, Media, and Toys & Collectibles. The way my inventory is actually stored utilizes even more sub-categories (in clothing, there are bins for Sweaters, Pants, Shorts, Kids' Clothing, Sleepwear, etc.) and is subject to change and become more granular as my inventory grows.

Here's how the Bread/Butter/Caviar situation shook out in 2019:

| ITEM TYPE | HOW MANY SOLD *(of 793)* | COST OF GOODS | GROSS SALES *(of $23,803.59)* |
|---|---|---|---|
| **Bread** (under $30) | 563 (71%) | $275.17 | $11,352.62 |
| **Butter** (between $30-$100) | 209 (26%) | $265.27 | $9,050.97 |
| **Caviar** (over $100) | 20 (2.5%) | $23.82 | $3,400.00 |
| | *Hours Worked: 692* | | *Wage: $34 + change/hour* |

That's why you can't hate on the Bread and Butter. This is also why, with a strong foundation of Bread and Butter, my aim going forward is to spend far less processing time to make more money on fewer items by really cultivating the Caviar in my store. The goal here is to continue to drive up my "hourly wage" and general income over time.

## DEFINING TREASURE

Don't throw the Bread and Butter out with the bathwater though! How's that for a malaphor? There is a lot of truth to the idea that the riches are in the niches, and some combination of education, intuition, and good fortune leads us into those niches. I've found that following my gut isn't just for therapeutic interventions—it's also handy for finding amazing items.

However, back to the aforementioned longevity strategy: a big, solid foundation is not easily or reliably built upon a few niche items. You can't make a living looking for needles in haystacks when you only get paid for the needles, not the looking. At least, I can't—it's not my business model. You can't eat bowlfuls of caviar for breakfast, lunch, and dinner, day after day, right? Firstly, where would you find all that caviar? How would you afford it? Secondly, ew.

If you're paying attention, you might be thinking, "Hey, wait a minute! What about the abundance mentality you had a couple of paragraphs ago?" To you, I say, "Touché." Here's the thing. This might mean we are arriving at the upper limit of my current level of enlightenment, and if so, I'll cop to that. In my experience so far, there are certainly great, high-quality, valuable items out there for the taking—but, with my particular strategy and the amount of time I am willing to invest in searching for said items, I don't find them every day. I don't find them every other day. In short, so far, I have not found them reliably and frequently enough to hang my hat on those kinds of items only. Does that mean I'm stuck selling Bread, Bread, and more Bread? Of course not. If anything, it means I've got plenty of room to grow into better inventory, perhaps eventually investing less time (but perhaps a little more money in terms of cost of goods), finding fewer items each time I go out sourcing, and over time, gradually improve the caliber of my store. That's actually a lot easier to do with a Bread-and-Butter-full store chugging away in the background. In fact, that is exactly my aim—working less for increased and more sustainable income, thereby having more and more time to enjoy and pursue the rest of life! Ah, but I'm getting ahead of myself.

# Chapter 7: Intangibles

## Nostalgia

The true value of most things, especially in the world of secondhand and vintage, lies in nostalgia. I've come to believe that nostalgia is king, because it encapsulates both collective and niche treasure. Sometimes, it's personal nostalgia, as I suspect is the case for the vintage knee hugger monkey in the Toys & Collectibles row of the Caviar table. I paid a dollar and one cent for that monkey (actually, I bought two for a dollar and one cent each), and someone was willing to pay over 200 dollars to buy it. Those are the facts.

My own personal speculation about the sale of this monkey is that it was probably just like one the buyer had as a child; they haven't been manufactured in ages, and they're rare in the wild. Perhaps the buyer's original monkey was misplaced in a move, destroyed somehow, or simply lost to time. Whatever the case, I suspect buyers who want a piece of their childhood more than they want a certain number of dollars (in this case, 200) are more than happy to pay the price. It's a worthy exchange, from both sides of the virtual cash register.

I also think personal nostalgia plays a salient role in gift giving —as a rule of personality, there is a pretty large chunk of our population made up of people who highly value thoughtful gift giving. What's more thoughtful than getting your sister an exact replica of her favorite stuffed monkey from 40 years ago, whose limbs you ripped off during a sibling brawl? Exactly. There is nothing.

There's also a whole world of collective nostalgia—this could be a certain design style, fashion, sturdiness, or other quality of yore. One of my favorite examples of this is the aforementioned Coogi sweater—such an iconic, unique, and instantly recognizable look. The nostalgia and cultural value attached to the Coogi is so strong, even non-Coogi brand sweaters will include the phrase "Coogi Style" in their listing titles. I'm sure those non-brand sweaters were designed and manufactured in the first place in an attempt to get in on the hot fashion trend of the day by emulating the features of the iconic Coogi, and now, decades later, they are still going for that same value-by-association. Well done, Coogi! That's some serious nostalgia-fueled brand power!

Another favorite and more recent example is a yardsale find— actually, five finds—for which I paid a dollar apiece. They were five toddler-size, severely ruffley, frilly vintage dresses. When I saw them, I didn't know anything about them (unlike the Coogi), but I noticed they looked legitimately vintage, based on the style and fabric, and that they seemed to be exquisitely detailed and well made, and well kept over the last four or five decades. I thought they were lovely, so I bought them. It wasn't until I got home and started researching the brand that I realized just what incredible treasures they were. Apparently, the brand was highly collectible. Dresses just like these (seemingly the smaller, the better) were selling for hundreds of dollars a piece.

I was shocked! I immediately logged, photographed, and listed all five. Within 30 minutes, the first one sold for 200 dollars. Within twelve hours, three more had sold for the same price, each! Boy, was I glad I had bought those dresses! That was the largest profit in the shortest time period in the history of my store. These dresses had massive nostalgic value, and to be honest, I still don't totally know why! Are they for real-life *Toddlers in Tiaras?* Are they clothing for really, really fancy dolls? Who actually wants them, and why? The world may never know.

I am wondering about the answers to those kinds of questions way more than I'm not wondering about them. Sometimes, it's perfectly obvious: consumers of all kinds look for the best price—I bought many Old Navy cardigans for a quarter and sold them for 7-20 bucks. It's cheap, and while Old Navy is already a fairly inexpensive brand, it tends to be consistent. People love their cardigans, even second-hand! Some even want one in every color. It's their thing. Another obvious one: collectors collect things. In every category in my store, I promise there are items that people will purchase in order to bolster their personal collections.

Sometimes, the reason people buy things has to do with a very narrow niche. Once I bought a bundle of 14 tiny straw hats made in Haiti for under 50 cents per hat. I thought they were cute, but after some research I realized that if I provided measurements for the brim and inside diameter of the hat, there was a good chance doll collectors would be interested in them. I listed them for only about

$14.99 each, multiple quantities available, and one person decided to offer me a hundred dollars for a bundle of several. That was a great sale for me early on in my store, and sure enough, the buyer wanted them—with extremely specific measurements—for several dolls in her collection!

One slight lean to the left of personal collections are personal connections—there's that nostalgia again! I mean like, really personal. My favorite example of a personal connection relates to *Hamilton* (the musical), which is my favorite musical of all time. Lin, you're my hero. I had a 2017 *Hamilton* official merchandise calendar listed in my store, in the original packaging and totally unused. The only problem was, this wall calendar was at least a whole year out of date: I didn't even list it during the year it was from. I seriously had my doubts about who would want this thing. I figured at best, some (fellow) rabid Hamilton fan would buy it to cut out the monthly images and plaster them all over their bedroom walls while singing along with the cast recording into their hairbrush or something. What actually happened was arguably *way* cooler.

A family member of one of the original cast members purchased it because they were so very proud of their family member starring in the role on Broadway. They wanted to collect a bunch of copies of the calendar so all their other family members could have one! I definitely screamed when I read the message from the buyer, who was kind enough to volunteer this information in a message to simply say thanks for accepting the offer they had submitted for this item. I was so excited to ship that outdated calendar! It sold for under 20 bucks, but it is undoubtedly one of my favorite sales ever.

Another common situation related to nostalgia is someone buying your item to replace an identical one they previously owned, like I speculated earlier about the knee-hugger monkey. In that case, I am indeed speculating, but just this week, a buyer mentioned to me that she was purchasing this teeny, tiny stuffed blue dog to replace a much-loved missing one from their household. I was so glad my teeny, tiny blue dog could stand in for the original, and I told her so. Sweet things like that happen all the time!

One simple reason people buy my stuff, from the totally obscure to the totally mundane, has to do with offering international shipping services. There might be identical items available from other sellers, but people will pay a premium if you're the only one willing to ship it internationally. This is one reason I am willing to ship almost anything internationally; the buyer still covers the cost of shipping, so it makes no difference to me!

Sometimes, items I sell are so weird, I can't even begin to guess why someone wanted them . . . but I'd bet a Coogi that whatever the particulars, their desires are rooted in nostalgia. I think of nostalgia in different degrees. I think of primary nostalgia as something we personally connect to because of first-hand experience, like the teeny tiny blue dog that was replacing it's identical twin. I think of secondary nostalgia as something we connect to in a more general way, like seeking out vintage kitchen wares from a certain design era because that's the style that we have personally chosen to identify with.

People have primary and secondary nostalgia for all sorts of things, it seems. I'm talking about stuff like outdated fashion (teacher vests, as I like to call them); broken stuff for parts or to fix; brandless, tagless stuffed animals . . . You can see why I frequently ask myself, "Who's willing to pay my asking price for this thing? Who wants it at all?" Perhaps the real question is, if it's so confounding, why are those kinds of items in my store? Well, frankly, everything is in there because when I found it, even having little knowledge of the item, I probably had a gut feeling that it might sell. Or at the very least, I was curious enough to take a chance on it and do a little experiment. It's definitely a chicken-or-egg situation—it's listed because it will sell, and it will sell because it's listed.

A final note about nostalgia: I feel that I now have my own personal tertiary nostalgia for many of the items I've mentioned in this chapter. I have this fun bank of experience with these items, the interesting ways I acquired them and the unusual profit margins or circumstances or buyers associated with their sales. There is now a special place in my heart that flutters a little when I see similar items out in the wild while I'm sourcing. This tertiary nostalgia is significant, because much of the time it compels me to buy those similar items. Whether a super valuable piece of vintage fashion or a 2017 Hamilton calendar that might sell for $20, if I see another one out there someday and the price is right, I'm totally buying it.

## So What?

The jury is definitely in on this one: Bread and Butter are delicious. Caviar is delectable. I've learned so much from mugs, books, shoes, and yes, even the *occasional* Beanie Baby. I sincerely can't wait to get to the end of the month to see my numbers. I still experienced pockets of doubt as I transitioned to full-time eBay work, and the subsequent income that goes along with more or less being a purveyor of nostalgia. I still have exceptional months, slow months, and many months in between.

Now more than ever, nostalgia is scooting over a little bit to make room for the values of sustainability and environmental awareness. I know some people might tune out at the mention of environmental issues, but tree hugging aside, that conversation has potentially massive implications for the second-hand market, of which my store is a part! I actually do really appreciate how the things I buy to resell are effectively rescued from the jaws of a landfill somewhere—or at least have the chance to re-enter the economy, get some more use, and postpone the trip to the trash can. It's not just me—other consumers are starting to be more concerned with this, too. There is a whole backlash against fast fashion on the rise, part and parcel with trendy minimalism and small business support. There is also a great design and fashion nostalgia sweet spot right now for all things housewares and clothing. There is widespread preference right now for all things shabby chic, vintage, and mid-century modern; tomorrow, there will probably be a new trend that's really just a nostalgic return to an old trend. It seems we really do find some kind of comfort in constant change.

A lot of people really do like the genuinely vintage: the arguably higher-quality materials and over-all heartier, better-made items of bygone eras. I count myself among those people; now, if I want something specific from an earlier time, I'm looking at eBay first! In fact, one of these days, I want to get my own Coogi, and I'm certain that if I can't find it in the wild, I'll find it on eBay in all of its second-hand glory.

I really do enjoy the ongoing treasure hunt, the changing tides, and endless entertainment for my endless curiosity. I didn't start this store just to buy a bunch of crap and set the whole thing on cruise control. I'm engaged with it, and so far, it's been a very enriching life experience and a great way to replace the income from my previous career, to boot.

I certainly can't tie up my inventory or my choices which have led to its vast and miscellaneous existence with a prim little bow. This whole thing is a work in progress. I'm still actively trusting my gut about things and integrating new knowledge as I go. The world of sourcing opens wide when you realize you are not necessarily your ideal customer—on the other side of the same coin, often my own taste and intuition pay off! All my favorite items, sold and unsold alike, have a couple things in common: I liked them, and I could easily imagine someone else liking them, too.

## LESS IS MORE

*I see her as soon as I walk through the door!* Batgirl. A gorgeous, 1997 life-sized cardboard cutout of Batgirl. She's folded in half next to the dingy beige metal shelves full of chipped glassware, outdated lamps, and a giant bin of mangled kitchen utensils. Five bucks. I snap a photo of her and immediately text it to my husband. "That's awesome! How much?" he fires back. "$5," I tell him. "Want me to grab it?" (I already have.) "Yes!"—got it. This is a stellar find, and yes, finding super awesome things for super cheap is a common workplace hazard for me. The good news is, there's treasure everywhere! The bad news is, there's treasure everywhere! The struggle is real sometimes. But surprisingly, and perhaps a little paradoxically, I've actually thinned out my collection of worldly possessions a good deal since starting this experiment over three years ago. I should point out that it's not been a totally linear path, paring things down. I've also beefed up a particular collection or two of my own; for example, there is a certain kind of vintage refrigerator magnet that I simply adore, so when I find them in the midst of sourcing for my store, I selectively add to that very specific collection. Even so, in terms of my general volume of personal possessions, it's something like seven steps forward, and the occasional half-step back.

The stuff I own has undoubtedly decreased, while the appreciation I have for the items that remain in my possession has increased. I think there are a few things at play in this correlation. For one thing, the simplicity of my stuff and my physical environment appeals to me more and more the longer I'm on this planet. I also have experienced my fair share of overwhelm when I have 300 eBay items to process strewn about my living room in various states of sorting. That kind of stresses me out for the moment and fuels my desire for the generally tidier space that awaits me on the other side of logging and moving all of it to the holding zone.

Another huge part of this less-is-more equation is that for me, being frugal isn't just about being cheap—it's about maximizing value. I want the stuff I own to be a 10/10 (or as close as possible) for goodness-of-fit in my budget, my environment, and my life. The more stuff I have, the more time I spend cleaning, organizing, and shuffling things around. Contrary to what you might think if you were a fly on my wall during a logging day, I am not actually on this earth for the sole purpose of shuffling things around. Therefore, I want to spend as little time as possible engaging in general maintenance of superfluous stuff.

That being said, being frugal is fun, and I do entertain the try-it-and-sell-it-if-it-doesn't-work-out method a good bit. If I'm not sure this white ceramic berry crate will be a 10/10 fit for my life and kitchen cabinet space, I have the luxury of buying it super cheap and trying it out for a few weeks. If it feels like clutter and gets in my way and never gets used the way I had envisioned, I can just list it, move it to inventory, and it will be on it's way out before long. Good try; better luck next time. No harm, no foul.

I also recently have implemented an exchange method for household items I may want to keep for myself, especially clothes. The current protocol is to bring home the item—that white ceramic berry crate, for example—and in order to integrate it into my kitchen cabinets, I have to swap out and immediately get rid of something else that's already wasting space in there. I can do whatever is appropriate for the swapped out item—throw it away, donate it, give it to a friend, or list it. This is really effective for me, because swapping items forces me to think differently than when I'm generally decluttering.

If the item I purchased to possibly keep for myself is clothing, I have to trade out *two* pieces of clothing to keep a single new piece. This is mostly because, despite my best efforts thinning out my closet, I still have way too many clothes that I hardly or never wear lurking in there. I think that during a big cleanout attempt, after 20 hangers or so, my brain shuts off. This two-for-one swap out has been very effective so far, and I plan to keep doing it until further notice.

As a side note, I also have been known to comb through my stuff to find a handful of items to list in my store when I am really close to hitting a certain number of new inventory items for the month. It's amazing how quickly and completely my attachment to many items can be reframed by this question: Which do I want more —this thing, or $25?

Another pillar of frugality for me is aligning my spending with my values—such as simplicity, goodness-of-fit, and high quality.

Since frugality itself is one of my values, gently used items tend to be a good option. Most items lose a lot of their original sticker-price retail value as soon as the box is opened or the tags are ripped off (ask any action figure collector). I am by no means an economist, but typically, paying a good (low) price for something desirable falls in line with my own values more so than the intrinsic value attached to having something "new." That's one reason I'll probably never buy a new car; I'll buy a very lightly used rental vehicle that was barely driven from the previous year or something, and pay fair market value for it, in cash if possible, but never straight off the new-car lot. It just doesn't line up with my values; I'm certainly not saying that you should have the same values as me, but I am saying you will probably have a less dissonant experience with the stuff you own and the money you spend if they both line up with your own values as much as possible.

## LITTLE BY LITTLE

So, what's it like gradually shaping myself and my lifestyle into this simpler, more frugal, values-based model? If you're looking for brutal honesty, I'll happily admit I could probably go through my belongings today, just like I did in the very beginning of my store and still find a bunch of things I'd be willing to part with. Maybe not quite as many, but I'm certain there would be some. Accumulating stuff is sneaky; consumerism is a big ship to turn, but I know I'm making progress.

As a former hobby thrifter, I see lots of things, frequently, that I'd like to buy for myself. In the beginning, this was very challenging; something that helped was changing my criteria for when I'd actually buy something for myself. In short, now I only buy something if I feel like it's exactly what I want. No compromises (usually—I do err). This might sound like a hard line to draw, but whether it's a sweater with a small hole I realistically wouldn't want to take the time to repair, or a cute coffee mug that's pretty similar to one I already have, I feel much better when I say no to those kinds of items now. It's more valuable for me to travel light in my life than it used to be. I'm not afraid anymore that I won't have enough. I don't need the dopamine hit of buying a new trinket to help me get by; there was a time when I truly did. A lot has shifted, but that's not to say I've arrived.

Kind of like how you don't have to start a business in one radical, risky leap, I also don't feel that people don't necessarily need to downsize their possessions in one manic decluttering session, ripping off the consumerism band aid. It can feel good to do that, but it can also allow us to avoid deeper changes we need to make within. There is so much power in intentionally becoming aware of and altering our relationship to things. For me, this continues to be a series of gradual, foundational changes: not the mere elimination of stuff.

Ever the experimenter, I'm always open to new ways of enjoying the journey as I continue to creatively minimize my stuff. Truly, this is a win-win situation for me, minimizing while building up an even-larger inventory. It's working really well so far, and as a bonus, I'm continuing to refine my relationship with stuff. I'm happy with that—I know it's totally okay to be right where I am, and these days, I am not inclined to rush through.

One thing I've learned about myself in the last few years is that while I love shoes, books, and teeny-tiny things, I also really, really love space. I'm not talking about the solar system here, people. I'm serious about this. Space is at least as valuable as most of the things we fill it with. And guess what? We already *know* this! And we know we know this, because we pay more money on airlines to have a roomier seat, higher mortgage payments for houses with larger and more numerous rooms, and even more for a computer with more "space" on it in the form of hard-drive storage. I probably don't even need to point out the space we acquire to house our actual stuff— storage units, basements, and attics overflow. In some ways, we prioritize space. In others, we prioritize stuff. We are paradoxes at best, hypocrites at worst.

Even in the decluttering, minimalizing trend in which we now find ourselves, it can be hard to consider parting with possessions. But I really want you to think about this for yourself for a moment. Consider it: what if the space—your experience of it, the extant availability of it—is actually more enjoyable and valuable than your stuff? Even just some of your stuff! What if space is one of the hottest commodities of all? What if that's true in your schedule? When is the last time you had a chunk of time, be it an hour or a week, with absolutely no scheduled activity, no to-do list, no obligations? How many of us don't even know what that feels like? What about mental, emotional and relational space? Room in your life for new people? What would it be like to have open space waiting—a standing invitation for new experiences, opportunities, or relationships? What if your inbox was at zero? There's a reason that feels good, and we can't chalk it all up to feeling accomplished and productive. We all are here, taking up some amount of space and time; and, we are attracted to possibility and anticipation. I want you to really, personally think about it. What would you like to make space for?

ANNA PACKER

# THE REWARDS

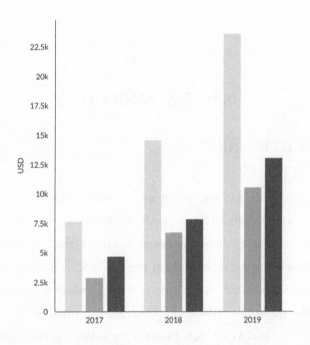

*How much do you make?*

## CHAPTER 8: ENOUGH

### PENNIES TO BENNIES

John and I used to joke that if we ever wrote or talked about about all this in any official form—podcast, blog, book, whatever—it would have to be called *Pennies to Bennies* because one of our favorite pastimes in selling on eBay is "turning a benny," a.k.a. "flipping a benny," a.k.a. making a $100+ sale on an item for which we paid up to one dollar per hundred dollars of profit. So, that could be something that costs $1 and sells for $101, or something that costs $3 and sells for $303, etc. It applies almost every time one of us makes back at least 100x what we paid for an item.

I couldn't bring myself to actually title this book Pennies to Bennies because it's so extraordinarily cheesy. It also just doesn't fully encompass what this book has come to represent; I hope by now it wont shock you when I say it's not all about the money. And while it's not all about the money, it is definitely kinda about the money, so if you don't mind, I'm going to talk about the money now.

This is actually what I believe everyone wants to know about the most, but few people feel comfortable overtly asking. I actually welcome money questions, and don't mind sharing my numbers at all! However, giving a specific dollar amount for an answer is a little tricky, because the store has been growing steadily the whole time I've been selling stuff. Go figure.

The simple answer is: I always make enough. That's the beauty of this whole thing. When it was part-time supplemental work, I made corresponding income. When I went all-in and worked full time, before long I started making full-time income. From there, I kept growing it, sometimes at a more intense rate of growth than other times, but growing all along. Now, thanks to reaching a critical mass in terms of my large inventory, I work part-time hours and still make a full-time income, even on the weeks or months I take off, thanks to the fruits of past labor.

Usually, when people ask "how much do you make," they aren't looking for a deep, historical explanation. So, when people ask about my income or sales in a real-time, present-day conversation, I usually describe in a nutshell the previous month, because that's a concise, current snapshot of how much I'm making at the time. A person who asks the same exact question six months down the road will get a totally different answer, I'm sure.

I'm going to give you a lot more than that kind of a snapshot here, because both the overview and the nitty gritty details of my store's performance provide important context. Truth be told, I've made a lot more that I even thought I could when I set out—I'm currently on track to make more than I made in my best year in private practice, even. And I'm not stopping there. My goals change. My expenses change. My pace of growth changes. In the spirit of talking money, let's examine some real numbers, change and all.

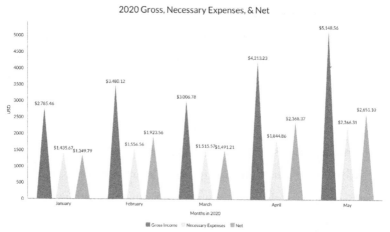

2020 Gross, Necessary Expenses, & Net

Based on past data and current plans for my inventory, I'm aiming to gross just north of $50,000 in 2020. That aim has borne out so far. My current model of workflow is a loosely month-on/month-off model. That's not to say it's 50/50 on and off; I still have more "on" months than "off" months so far.

An "off" month is a month in which I am not really building my inventory—maybe just keeping up with listing enough to replenish my active listings by replacing the ones that sell during the month with new listings. A few listings here, a few listings there. Maybe one full day a week, maybe not even! Maybe several weeks in which I only shop (if I feel like it) and ship things out (whether I feel like it or not). During an "off" month, I usually extend my handling time to take a full-on break if I'm traveling or if I just straight up want to spend less of my time shipping stuff. An "off" week might require anywhere from zero hours to maybe five hours of eBay work for the whole week, including only shipping and elective shopping; extrapolated to an "off" month, that's about 20 hours of work if I'm actually at home to ship and my handling time stays relatively normal.

An "on" month is more like 20+ hours a week (still not usually a traditional full-time workload, mind you) and could even be 40-60 hours per week if I'm really building up my inventory or shopping

## First 3 Months vs Last 3 Months

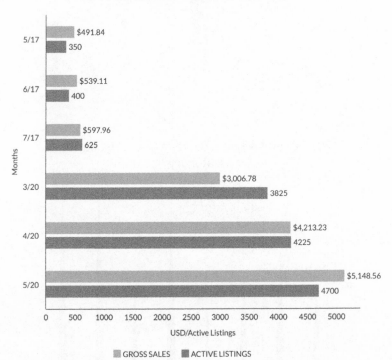

like a maniac, or massively reorganizing the garage or something. Even in those busy weeks, I get to decide when it's too much, and I can stop at any point. I rarely do, but having the freedom to is borderline intoxicating. This whole model developed out of the estimates of how much time it actually takes me to process items in a

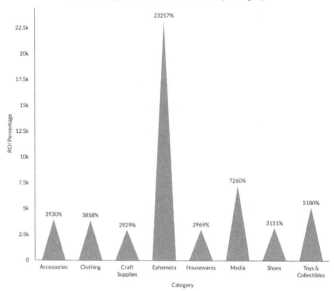

2020 Average Return on Investment by Category

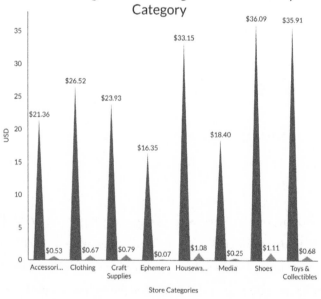

2020 Average Sale & Average Cost of Goods by Category

one-month period if everything proceeds typically. Thanks to tracking my hours, I have almost three years of data to prove to me how much time it takes to process items through various stages, so that helps me have a reasonable template to work with when I'm planning my month.

If you're not as much of a data nerd as I am, fear not. You can still be successful without having to be terribly meticulous. eBay actually has a pretty good analytics setup to give you information about your sales and general store performance (how many returns, what kind of feedback you're getting from buyers, etc.), so you can look at the back end of your store anytime and typically see up to 90 days of data for most things and never fill a single cell in an independently-maintained spreadsheet like I do. As long as you have a profitable business (making more money than you're spending) and you're happy with the performance of your store, I think tracking the details is mostly optional. For me, the details are essential, but they might not be for everyone.

If you think you might be somewhere in the middle regarding interest or follow-through with collecting and utilizing data about your store, I say there's no harm in starting a spreadsheet with all the things you think you'll be interested in and simplifying it later. For example, in the first month or two of listing in my store, I kept track of how many items sold via Best Offer versus Buy It Now. Soon, I realized I didn't actually care about that, and promptly quit tracking it after those first couple of months.

I love numbers because (duh) they tell a story. My numbers have gotten better as I've become more experienced, and I don't just mean I've made more profit. I have, but other stuff about the story has improved along the way, too. For example, in my first December

(2017), typically the hottest selling month of the year, I sold 54 items. My cost of goods was 82 cents per item (total of $44.28 for the month), and my average selling price was $21.79. My gross profit that month was $1,176.58. That was the first time I grossed over a thousand dollars in one month! Cut to this past December (2019), I sold 106 items. My cost of goods was 62 cents per item (total of $65.72 for the month), and my average selling price was $36.78. My gross profit that month was $3,898.83.

Incremental improvements in the processes of sourcing and listing have contributed greatly to more than tripling my gross sales. Let me show you what I mean. If the metrics I just mentioned—number of items sold, cost of goods, and average selling price—had merely doubled in volume, December 2019 very well might have looked like this: 108 items sold, cost of goods 82 cents per item (total of 88.56), and average selling price $21.79, totalling $2,353.16 in gross sales. Instead, I got better at running my store (paying less for better quality items in larger volume) and made an additional $1,500+ on almost the same number of items! Even if I did (finally) receive my Hogwarts letter, I don't know that I could give this kind of magic up. Just for kicks, here are my current all-time monthly averages:

## MAY 2017–MAY 2020

| |
|---|
| Average Gross Sales: $1,429.69 |
| Average Number of Items Sold: 53 |
| Average Cost of Goods: $45.63 |
| Average Necessary Expenses: $777.58 |
| Average Net Profit: $956.27 |

For the sake of transparency and pure, unadulterated love of storytelling numbers, here are a few more details on my 2020 eBay Store so far; the cutoff is May 2020 for a couple of reasons. It's three years to the month since my store first began operating officially with more than hobbyist intentions driving it. Plus, I *really* want to wrap up this book draft before I turn 30 in June. Just being real.

A lot washes out in the means—but that's kind of the point. It's a steady business, whether it's mid-growth spurt or mid-month "off." In case you are curious (ahem, John) this little one-person eBay operation has turned exactly thirty-one bennies to date. But as we have established, man cannot live on Caviar alone, turning bennies night and day. Those bennies account for only 4% of the all-time gross sales of my store! Regarding the data I've shared so far, my store has included over 7100 active listings and grossed $64,384.24. I've been electively full-time on eBay for eight months, and I'm more aware than ever that the best is yet to come.

For my fellow number lovers and bonafide data nerds, I've included a bunch more charts and tables in the appendix of this book just for you. From this point on, I'm zooming back out of the performance data details and shifting my magnifying glass to the details of personal impact and implications. If you're not into that, feel free to peruse the appendix and rejoin me when you're able. I'll be right here.

## Mo' Money, Mo' Problem Solving

The state of my store as of now is still more full-time than not. Currently, I want to aggressively destroy my student-loan debt (also a

work in progress, furthered by the proceeds from this very book—
thank you!), so I probably won't be doing very many five-hour work
weeks this year. However, that's my prerogative, and if anything
comes up that I decide needs to take a higher priority than my goal of
eradicating my student-loan debt, I reserve the right to change my
mind and shift my work accordingly.

By now, you probably get that I genuinely like work—
especially  hard work. John actually teases me about this and
sometimes bluntly encourages me to slow my roll because he sees that
I need to before I see that I need to. Thanks, John! I don't have any
chill to speak of, really. Sure, I like to have fun, I like to relax on
vacation, but my default mode is to work. And start projects. And
spin plates. And iterate. And finish projects. I love the thought that
the hard work I'm doing at the moment will pay me handsomely,
both now and later, whenever I do periodically relax, take little
sabbaticals, visit my friends and family, work intensively on creating
new things, and clock in and out of my other jobs.  By other jobs, I
mean projects, freelance gigs, and anything else that I deem to be
legitimate work, whether I'm paid for it now or later, in cash or fresh
eggs or gratitude. If that definition of work sounds a little bit all over
the place, that's because it is. This is why I use an hours tracker,
people.

Incidentally, after a couple months of having the basic, free
version of my hours tracker app, I actually did pay for a one-time
upgrade so that I could have *unlimited* jobs. (Insert facepalm here.)
You're welcome to judge me for having so many jobs, but in any case,
I love being able to track them all and work harder or prioritize better
when I need to, as well as to look at the time I've already put in to

slow down guilt-free and repeat one of my favorite reminders: I've done enough.

The line between hustle and grind is a fine one. That's one reason I tend to set inventory goals rather than sales goals, because inventory is the side of the business I have some semblance of control over. Another reason it's complicated to answer questions about how much money I actually make because the model is always changing, in both calculated and uncalculated ways. I make all kinds of willful adjustments, of course, but life has a way of indiscriminately throwing wrenches toward all the moving parts.

## WRENCHES

The thing about wrenches is that if implemented correctly, they can fix things, but when carelessly thrown, they can wreck things. I've got a handy example of a recent one—a wrench in its own right which also happens to part of a recurring sequence of similar wrenches: the kind that hits me square in the planner. Let me tell you about this particular wrench.

My goal in January 2020 was to add 600 things to my store before February. My years of data informed my prediction that I'd sell about 100 items during January, which turned out to be right on. But an unexpected thing happened—I got through sourcing and logging, and was just starting to photograph my way through about 500 items when I suddenly left my home for a week. One of my family members had an emergency up north, and I was able to accompany her on a trip to tend to said emergency. So I wound up spending a week 1,200 miles away from my piles of yet-to-be-processed stuff. Yeesh. I was so utterly grateful to have the flexibility to jump into the car and support my family during such a critical time, but as for getting 500 things listed in the short span of 3 weeks, two of which were already bygone? *Ce n'est pas* possible.

My store still made plenty while I was gone; all my listings were running extended-handling time, so I didn't think about it again until my feet were back on Southern soil. That detachment was such a luxury, but to be honest, it also totally threw me off. I had a huge pile of stuff still waiting to be processed by the end of the month, and the only reason I got around to listing 200 of them in January is because I outsourced some work for the first time *ever!*

Talk about perfect timing. I wound up giving a couple batches of items that needed to be photographed to my first-ever contracted helper, Watson. Without him, I would have certainly been stuck in the photographing bottleneck, lucky to get 50 items listed by February. For you non-number people, 50 is way less than my original goal of 500. I am so grateful for Watson and his impeccable timing, and even with the extra help from Watson, my dreams of pushing hard for 600 items (a net increase of 500) in January were crushed, and I honestly felt like I had really failed, hard. Failing for good reasons, it seems, still feels like failing. However, not even getting close to my goal definitely gave me some rich tape to review to see what I might learn from missing a huge goal by a country mile. It also helped me refine my assessment of just how much failure had actually occurred.

In retrospect of that January, I quickly realized it was no wonder I felt like I had failed and wasn't doing enough! I had the best-laid plans of rocketing through my last batch of 500 items to build my inventory up to this never-before-attained 4k-item baseline. Four thousand items was to be the solid ground upon which I started my first month-on/month-off experiment. So, there were stakes. Ok, fine. Makes sense. What really got me thinking, though, was that I had prioritized something over my original goal. Because I could!

I had some working-through to do about the beautiful dialogue between my sense of flexibility and my sense of discipline. I had really seen this dialogue in action, but this time, the real-life consequence was that I simply could not meet my original goal in its original time frame. What was I to do? Kick the pressure into high gear, knowing I perform fairly well under pressure, and just bear down on myself until I hit my goal, better-late-than-never style? That's a common approach for me, but it usually comes from my sense of discipline vetoing my sense of flexibility. So after some consideration and consultation, I decided to do something different. I don't want deadlines to crush me, perhaps especially not self-imposed ones. I don't want to set unrealistic goals and expectations, but I certainly did want to get to 4k items as quickly as possible and keep building my store.

So, I decided to chunk my on/off months based on the actual number of items I could reasonably process in the expected timeframe (usually, a month), but the kicker is, the timeframe is secondary now. If I blast through my listing goal in two weeks, I might take two extra weeks off, or at least go easy on them, because I've objectively done enough already. If I don't quite make it to my listing goal by the end of the month, I can extend my self-imposed deadline: no harm, no foul. My next step will be to let it go and start over with a new goal at the start of a new month. What I definitely don't do is shame myself until the first of the month rolls around, cut out all rest and relaxation, or cancel other plans until I reach my listing goal.

My whole model has changed for the better. What that meant for January 2020 was that instead of running myself into the ground at the altar of preserving my original goal, I'd give myself two extra weeks—one week to make up the week I was away, one week for grace. My inventory goals got back on track, and my mindset around pushing myself, setting goals, and continuing on this fun and fascinating ride was in a much more constructive place, too. This time, the wrench definitely had a wrecking effect, but the wreck had a fixing effect.

Now I look back at January 2020 and see a lot more than I saw as I was living it. I realize now that the priorities of supporting my family members and using my flexibility as a resource, were very aligned with my values. That month was also the one-year anniversary of my Aunt Patti's death and the three weeks I spent in St. Louis/Illinois when she was in the hospital fighting for her life. So, probably for many reasons, driving up north a year later under somewhat similar circumstances to be supportive to my family was rightfully pretty dang important to me. I felt like it was what I needed to do, and I don't take those imperatives lightly.

## Pulling the Trigger

Allow me to take a moment to tell you a little more about hiring Watson to take photos for the first time during this whole January situation. This was a huge deal for me. In a way, the prospect of paying someone to help me with the more bottleneck-prone aspects of running my store was a wrench in and of itself. It didn't have to become a wrench, but it did because I was indecisive and risk-averse about it for so long. For months leading up to this point, I had hemmed and hawed about when, who, how much to pay, what kinds of items to entrust to a contractor, and blah, blah blah, blah blah for months before I even met Watson. I had even asked friends to keep their eyes peeled for good candidates, but nothing ever really materialized. I was hesitant; I didn't feel ready. It was starting to feel more like a problem to avoid than an opportunity to grow.

I had a realization in mid-January that unlike many puzzling problems I'd tinkered with and attempted to solve, I had only discussed the idea of hiring some help with John and a couple of my friends, wrestled with it in my mind, but never actually prayed about it. Never once asked God to put the right person in my path. As soon as I realized that, I promptly asked, and no joke: about 10 minutes later, Watson and I were having a conversation about it. I'm serious. You may not be the praying type, but it's a solid truth in relationships that usually, you don't get what you don't ask for! Asking makes all the difference.

When Watson expressed some interest in taking photos for my store, I had to finally, after much sporadic rumination, nail down a job description and terms. I had to think once and for all through things like paying by the hour versus paying by the item (how much per item and how many at a time), the level of independence and flexibility (coming to my house to take photos versus a portable batch of items to be photographed at his place on his time by a certain deadline), as well as specific preferences and tips for taking photos that are up to my standards, among other things. These were some of the important details that had become entangling weeds for me; it felt great to finally sort them out!

We went with a portable batch (typically 50 items at a time), for which Watson is paid a dollar per item, and we decide on a deadline that works for us both on a batch-by-batch basis. He actually picked up his first batch of 50 items from my front porch while I was on the road heading north in early January. In the beginning, I have to admit, I was holding my breath. I finally ironed out the details and committed to a trial period with Watson. But what if he hated it, and never wanted to do it again after a batch or two or eleven or eight? I had those fearful thoughts, but I went for it anyway. It's been working really well so far. Watson is a fast and effective photographer, so he probably makes $15-20 in his downtime, which is a pretty great, flexible part-time gig, if I do say so myself. I have no shortage of new drafts to list, even if I haven't photographed an item myself in months. Keep up the good work, Watson!

While I had to spend a little extra risk and bandwidth, onboarding the first-ever contract helper for my eBay store, I'm so grateful that in the fast-moving, last-minute trip planning, I found myself at this fork in the road: either quit thinking in circles about it and just pull the trigger, or wait until I get back to sort it all out, and oh by the way, Rambo my way through the remaining process for 600 new items all by myself. Something told me to just go for it, and I'm so glad I did! Watson's help has been worth every penny I've paid him and more (sometimes I throw in baked goods), and it's grown my business far beyond helping me catch up in January and February of 2020. It's one of the best triggers I've pulled in this business!

January 2020 was a critical time of little adjustments, rolling with the punches, trusting my store to keep going, and putting my head down to list once I got back home and into my groove. The time I lost was made up before long, and everything ultimately worked out. Another subtle change that month was my beginning to co-work once a week with my friend, Rachel. We both wanted to be less isolated and bored by the tedium that sometimes characterizes editing photos for her, and turning eBay drafts into listings for me. This is another thing I had really wanted to improve, but didn't know where to start. I had been somewhat bored and lonely at times, and I had spent too many days in sweatpants on my couch, listing, thinking about how much I would appreciate a change of scenery, an actual outfit, perhaps a latte, and some company with a like-minded hard worker who also had a bunch of busy work or tedious tasks to get done.

Rachel has been an amazing coworker for me, and I've really been enjoying our mutually productive, fun times together (which unfortunately came to a hard stop when the COVID-19 pandemic really ramped up in the US, but I'm confident we'll get back to coworking before we know it!). Plus, Rachel introduced me to the Great British Baking Show—but that's just the icing on the Bakewell tart.

Through all of these wrenchy situations, I'm learning that I often identify the problem long before I work up a plan (not to mention necessary chutzpah) to try a solution. I hope that these stories about wrenches can serve as a friendly reminder that change is challenging, and that's perfectly okay. Sometimes things need to marinate in my brain (and in yours), stars need to align, and opportunity needs a little time to come knocking. It's okay to wait on those things, but I have to watch out so I don't get stuck in a holding pattern for too long. I have learned to whistle while I work, and work while I wait. There is a time for every part of the process, so I'm doing my best to welcome each one. Resistance, as they say, is futile.

## KEEP THE CHANGE

I'm going to pass the mic to my inner psychology/therapy nerd for a bit, because there is so much goodness beyond the bottom line when it comes to growing an eBay business, and she especially wants to make sure you know all about that goodness. My life and my eBay store have both changed a lot over the last three years; this is no accident. While my whole business is built on slow, steady, hard work; all the blood, sweat, tears, time, dollars, and garage space I've invested into my business are grounded in the fundamental truth that it's okay to change. It's okay to change my mind, it's okay to change my plan, it's okay to pivot. You may have cringed when you read the word "pivot" just now—I get it, I'm a little buzzword-phobic myself. However, I can appreciate this one, because I've found that I don't have to stick with the decisions my past-self made in every single situation.

In my case, and probably in yours, the past-self has limited information; sure, she made the best decision she could using what information and experience and options were available to her at the time. That was then; this is now. I am allowed to scribble in a new path based on new information from new experiences and the ever-changing environment I live in. I am even allowed to straight-up just change my mind! Imagine! This is the tricky thing about experience being the best teacher: sometimes you learn that what you chose is not the right thing at all, not the right thing anymore, or not the right thing forever. As a child, I was taught not to be a quitter. I still don't want to be a quitter—unless quitting is actually the responsible, ethical, vital thing to do.

If I'm growing and changing, doesn't it make sense that the thing chosen by my past-self might not be the best for my present-and/or future-self? Some things we grow into, some things we grow out of, some things grow with us. It's not a one-size-fits-all situation. Maybe it's messy or inconvenient; entertain it anyway. Don't knock it 'til you try it, if it lines up with your values and your dreams.

## RELENTLESS (SOMETIMES)

One little paradox that periodically pops up in my eBay business is the pairing of relentlessly going all-in with deploying discretion. These ideas sound like opposite approaches, but actually can be used simultaneously. Very often, all-in pertains more to attitude or approach about doing the overall thing, and discretion pertains to actions and behavioral choices while shopping, photographing items, and accepting Best Offers from buyers. Motivations also play a role here. Discretion seated in fear can serve me very differently than discretion seated in wisdom. If my all-in mentality comes from carelessness or foolishness rather than a deep belief in or commitment to success, I might run my whole store into the ground in short order.

If I asked you whether wisdom is better than fear, or whether commitment is better than carelessness, I'm sure you could tell me the obvious answer. However, rooting my attitude and behavior in wisdom and commitment is much easier said than done. This is one of my favorite flavors of humble pie; I get continual chances to examine myself and see where my motivations lie, as well as where and how these seemingly contrary concepts apply.

Speaking of checking my motivations, when I think back to my path through college and choosing a career, I notice now that I oscillated between people pleasing (because I wanted to prove I was smart and capable) and rebelling (because I wanted to be independent and do things in unorthodox ways). Stripping away some of my professional identity has shifted that momentum in some pretty surprising ways. Now, when it comes to my work, I notice I enjoy being smart and capable without having to prove it to myself or others (no as much, anyway—I'm only human). I don't have to rely on my degree or my caseload or my most recent training conference to lend credence to my work. That's downright refreshing. Not to mention, I carry some inner independence, even whenI have the occasion to work for someone besides myself.

It's not very often that I do work for someone else, but even when I'm volunteering or collaborating, I don't feel the need to rebel in order to preserve my independence or quirky approaches. These shifts didn't come by measuring out the exact center point between the extremes of people-pleasing and rebelling—I just needed to allow myself to grow healthier and more comfortable in my own intrinsic identity—i.e. I am not [just] what I do.

I've really been practicing one particular balancing act lately: discipline and flexibility, the pair that had me spinning out in late January. The tug-of-war over doing enough. A sure-fire path to feeling like I haven't done enough is when the sales are barely trickling in for a few days; Discipline stars telling me all kinds of paranoid stories about how I jumped the gun, bit off more than I could chew or didn't think something (or, the entire running-an-eBay-store thing) through, and how I'd better get to work. Flexibility tells me to chill, because all the goals and deadlines are self-imposed anway; loosey-goosey is so uncomfortable for me, though. When Discipline is louder, Flexibility feels like a flaky, flowery teenager who doesn't understand priorities or willpower. When Flexibility is louder, Discipline seems like an unreasonably cranky vice principal who is totally missing the point of living! This one I expect to be wrestling with for years to come.

As a sort of adapted-type-A person, under certain circumstances, I can flip on the discipline switch, put my head down and get it done at all costs. In perhaps a more natural and less stressed state, I am inclined to be flexible! I love it when I have the luxury of being flexible, but I also expect a lot from myself all of the time. Honestly, I am probably a little bit addicted to productivity. I'm always thinking several turns ahead of where I currently am on my route when I'm driving, but I also like to explore and find new routes altogether.

These parts of me certainly war with each other, and sometimes running the eBay store provides a Colosseum-like venue for them to duke it out. Sometimes one side wins, sometimes the other side wins. Should I be flexible, or should stick to my original word? Should I keep taking photos, come hell or high water, until this whole batch of items is done and subsequently feel very accomplished and glad to be through it, or should I admit I bit off more than I can chew, save the rest for tomorrow, and actually relax for the rest of the day, because I already clocked plenty of work hours? Both are valid, and really, since there are no stringent deadlines in listing on eBay, neither is necessarily wrong. Both are neutral. I don't actually know the answer to this yet; I've only gotten as far as trying to observe myself wrestling with these options to decide what's more in line with my priorities and values at the time. This is one of those blessing-curse combos that comes with being totally self-directed as a business owner/operator; it's a privilege to be in the position to be frustrated by it.

## WHIRLWIND

One of the things I found myself saying frequently in 2019—the year everything changed for me—was that life had been a whirlwind. I'd say this in conversation when people asked me how I was, when I plopped down on the couch in therapy, when I occasionally caught my breath, when I was sitting on the beach in California, when I was stuck in Atlanta traffic. All. The. Time. It just really felt like a whirlwind; obviously, that was the only fitting way to describe it. As you might imagine, I was very busy, but it was more than just busy. It was jam-packed. It was full of the unknown. It was beginnings and endings. It was change upon the winds, whirling around. Get the picture? What's interesting is that my present-day life also contains many of these same elements: fullness, unknowns, changes, travel plans, life stuff. And I love it. It's not a whirlwind anymore, because there's no chaos. It's not boring, because it's meaningful and miscellaneous.

While I love getting in the details and neurotically updating my spreadsheets, my allegiance is not actually to the bottom line. My passion for doing this, thinking about it all the time, and now writing about it, comes from the big picture: a project-based lifestyle, seeking my destiny, spending as much of my life in the best and highest ways I can. The big picture keeps me from feeling wishy-washy in the duller moments, and it's certainly not about being legalistic. Running this little resale business, from shopping to shipping, is not about cheapness—it's about value. Do I want a low cost of goods? Sure, but

I want to be interested in the goods, too. Do I want to find high-quality items? Yes, but not just for the sake of my store—it's for the sake of my quality of life.

## NO WASTE

I was talking with my own therapist one day (Anne, what's up?!), most certainly whingeing (not a typo) about the emotional perils of shifting from being a respected, educated member of the helping profession to—I don't know, yardsaling? She asked me if I'd ever bought something on eBay that I couldn't get anywhere else—of course I had! And, she wondered, wasn't that thrill of the treasure, the nostalgia, something I appreciated? Indeed, it was.

Running a private therapy practice and running an online resale shop are apples and oranges, but this was the first time I considered that there might be a valid crossover here. I still get to provide something helpful to people: that perfect one-of-a-kind treasure nostalgia. This cracked open my view a little bit more, helping me to realize that "helping others" still counts when it's outside the helping professions. And it doesn't just-barely count, it actually matters. And that's valuable. Just like showing up in my own life and being myself is valuable. If selling old stuff on eBay is an honest-to-goodness path leading in that direction, I'm in. More than that, I'm happy to be here.

There is a lot I've grown to love as I've worked to show up and be myself in my own life. I love being scrappy, using my still-developing skill sets, working from home, keeping stuff out of the landfills, and playing a small role in giving items extended life while their new owners enjoy deep nostalgic and/or functional satisfaction.

I love the prospect of overcoming my student-loan debt once and for all. For a long time, that seemed impossible.

As I reflect on the slow growth of this little quirky eBay store that occurred mostly on the sidelines and in the background until very recently, I'm proud that I chose this less-traveled path over the one I'd previously chosen. In my view, the previous path included some inevitable degree of decline in the quality of care for my clients and myself. It was a hard choice, but I have never been more certain that this was the right choice, ultimately benefiting all of us. I may go back to practicing psychotherapy someday; it was a great passion of mine for many years. If I do, I know this eBay experience will make me an even more compassionate and creative therapist, just like running my own psychotherapy practice informed starting a second successful business that has human behavior and relational implications all over it! It turns out, nothing is wasted after all.

## COMMUNITY

Another kind of wealth I've been building is a wealth of community. I cannot stress enough the importance of community, consisting of all kinds of characters in every part of the story—not the least of which are my virtual mentors and fellow scavengers over at The Scavenger Life. I feel like I was absolutely meant to find this community, and I feel so fortunate that I was able to find it remotely through Jay and Ryanne, who were putting out free and accessible content out of the goodness of their hearts and perhaps their own desire for community.

I've also connected with other like-minded people; one of my favorite connections is actually a re-connection. Dylan is a friend of mine from childhood, and it turns out that he also runs a full-time eBay store a short distance from where we grew up! I had no idea, for years! He's younger than me and has an even bigger, longer-running store than mine. I was thrilled to find out about this, and now we regularly compare notes and celebrate wins with each other. Just the other day, he texted me, "So…I sold something. I need someone to be stoked with me. You in?" And of course, I was totally in. He sent me a picture of this awesome thing he sold for a lot of money, and many fun emojis were exchanged. It's a blast!

Aside from all my fellow resellers, there is a lengthy curtain call to applaud, from my husband who is my long-time treasure-hunting partner and the designer of this sick book cover, to my dad who graciously edited my manuscript, to my family and friends who have donated inventory to my store and encouraged me, the vendors and shop owners and yardsale sellers I buy from, and so many more!

It's fun to think about and appreciate the role of community in getting an operation like mine up and running. I don't mind giving examples; I generally feel squirmy about giving totally unsolicited advice, but I do want to strongly encourage you to consider your community. If you are doing something new—anything new—do what you can to put yourself in the position to seek, recognize, and connect with people who will support you. I'm probably not changing the world with my eBay store, but my world has changed radically, and because of that, now more than ever I feel that I have so much to give and share, and I'm not too drained to put it out there. That was simply not available to me during much of my previous career.

Before wrapping up this bit about the importance of community, I want to linger here for a moment, to give one special shout out. January 7, 2020, one of my best and smartest friends who just wrote his fourth book, *Making Remote Work Work*, texted me "Why don't you literally write a book on your ecommerce trajectory? Seriously, that would be invaluable."

I don't know what it was about that text, but I instantaneously realized that, seriously, he was right! I've had hundreds of conversations with people about how all this works, at parties and rehearsals and the grocery store and auctions and weddings—all of that flashed into my mind when I read Gil's text, and in a flurry, I feverishly composed an outline over the next couple of hours. It's still hard for me to wrap my mind around, and yet I can't believe this idea didn't occur to me sooner.

I know some people are only mildly curious about my store; most people aren't likely to follow in my footsteps the way I've followed in the footsteps graciously illustrated by the Scavenger Life community. I realize that sharing this life experience with other people won't help everyone step-for-step. More importantly though, I believe sharing my experiments, creative work, and this whole way of being in the world is helpful to others in a big way. When we are living free and fulfilled, it helps. When we are making and keeping space for that which is most important, it helps. When we are showing up to our lives as ourselves, it helps. The more whole-hearted, healthy, and creative we can be, the better off we all are.

# CHAPTER 9: AND THEN SOME

## GROWING UP

Remember that time I told you I saved some of the sordid details of my backstory for later? Welcome to later, where I'm going to talk about some pre-2016 stuff. Some growing-up stuff. I'm getting personal because, call me crazy, running a lifestyle-altering business feels kind of personal to me. Not to mention, I am a Licensed Professional Counselor who practiced effective counseling and therapy for many years. I'd wager that most other therapists would agree with me that background matters. Family of origin matters. Childhood matters. Early experiences matter. How we think about work, money, debt, responsibility, and the availability of options matters. So bear with me as I stop off here for a little while, because this place is the origin of all those things.

As it turns out, I lived a whole life leading up to here-and-now, complete with K-12 and secondary education, moves, divorces, marriages, a bunch of parents and siblings, cats, and ferrets. You read that right. Ferrets. At least, one. At most, six. They are loads of fun, and I am determined to adopt another one someday and call him Peeve, just so I can introduce him as my pet, Peeve. (Thanks to my friend Connor for that brilliant idea).

So, I grew up in Illinois in a small town, off and on farms, writing songs, playing in the marching band, singing madrigals, performing in theater productions, running around the countryside with my friends, hanging out with my family, occasionally popping over to St. Louis for a taste of a real city, and figuring that just like most of my peers and both of my parents, I'd grow up and leave my little bubble someday for the exciting new frontier of college.

I had my share of challenges and traumas, but on the whole, I feel like I had a fairly typical midwestern modern upbringing. Based on my favorite activities, I figured, perhaps a little bit secretly, that either my girl band, Rosy, would majestically take off and I'd worry about college later, or I would audition for a college choir and marching band, somehow come up with my own euphonium to bring along with me, and major in some kind of music performance. I didn't want to be a music teacher, but I loved music, from playing brass singing motets to writing harmony-rich pop songs. On one hand, I had this fantasy about what life after high school would be, and on the other—the hand that dealt in reality—I had a lot of fear and doubt.

These fears and doubts may even sound familiar to you: I'm not good enough. I'll never make the groups I audition for. There are so many other people who are better than me at the things I want to do, so why bother? I can't possibly make a living being a musician, and there's no way I'll ever belong to the elite group at the height of musicianship. What will people think if I major in music? Who do I think I am? What if I fail? What will my parents say?

So, I chickened out. The auditions came and went. I didn't even try. Fortunately for me, I already loved the college I would be enrolling in for undergrad, so I knew I felt at home there, and I knew there would be something for me, surely! I was beyond ashamed that I had chickened out of pursuing what I felt for a long time was my purpose in life, but the "reasonable adult" part of my psyche (that was demanding more and more air time in my conscious mind that first semester of college) insisted that I had done the right, reasonable, and responsible thing by not majoring in music.

## COLLEGE

During my freshman year of college, I had Dr. Cameron for Psych 101, and something inside me felt a twinge of recognition. I could love psychology, I thought! After all, I was endlessly curious, very social, and increasingly analytical. Hadn't I so thoroughly enjoyed researching every detail I could dig up on mass murderer Richard Benjamin Speck for my senior English class paper in high school? This could be a good fit. I soaked up the course content and declared psychology as my major pretty quickly after that class, because, hey, this was a whole wide world that seemed like it could hold my interest for at least a few decades. Even then, the miscellaneous nature of the broad, diverse field of psychology appealed to me, almost more than any other quality. I knew I would never be bored, and I was thrilled by the very prospect.

Psychology in the context of criminality was definitely my favorite sub field, so for good measure, I simultaneously completed a

B.A. in psychology and a B.S. in criminal justice. I loved this subject matter, and I loved my internship in the mental health department of a state-run women's prison. To this day, that was one of my favorite clinical experiences ever, and I was just a lowly undergraduate intern, observing and doing busy work more than anything else.

I was loving psychology, and meanwhile, still struggling with my chickening-out of music. I felt totally unworthy. Like a lame, crappy hobbyist. I had no faith in myself or my abilities, and I mostly shut entirely down from music. There were times I would play and sing with my guitar or keyboard in my dorm, and I was definitely singing at the top of my lungs for the entire duration of the six-hour drive between my dorm and my mom's house a couple of states away. In a way though, I couldn't face myself. It was all or nothing, and since I already put the kibosh on all, I pretty much left myself with nothing.

Another little complication cropped up in the middle of my journey through undergrad. I was borrowing just enough money to cover part of tuition, books, room and board. I had a partial scholarship, but I went to a private school (read: e-x-p-e-n-s-i-v-e), and for a kid with no money, any amount was a lot. All in all, my undergrad loans put me in debt between forty and fifty thousand dollars. That's not even the complication.

As I learned more about my field, I heard over and over again that if I wanted to make "real money," I basically had to get another degree, like, a bigger and better one. Master's at least, Ph.D. (or PsyD) if possible, and typically, most people in psychology wound up doing three separate programs before arriving at a terminal degree. I could be in school full time anywhere from two to ten more years if I wanted a "real" psychology career. Any path would take a lot more work, and a lot more debt, because as I worked my way through undergrad by tutoring, doing desk jobs, babysitting, and numerous other gigs, I was barely getting by. I wasn't really too worried about the huge workload of more education; I was a pretty good student, and frankly, a pretty high-octane person accustomed to lots of ongoing hard work. I should have been more concerned about the prospect of more debt, but it didn't really sound like I had many options. The burden of student loan debt was totally normalized or altogether avoided in most conversations about further education. The emphasis was always on doing more good, helping more people, having a more prestigious career, and making more money as people called you "doctor." The way it seemed to me at the time, I could either live in a cardboard box with my bachelor's in psychology or double (or triple) down on my debt and come out the other end with a better title, more opportunities, more meaningful work, and a grown-up salary. It was pretty clear which was the better choice.

For a hot second, I did consider a career in criminal justice, but my then-boyfriend-now-husband (who, incidentally, was an actual professional musician in a touring rock band with exactly zero dollars of student-loan debt) shut that down pretty quickly. He just couldn't see five-foot-two me working as a correctional officer in a prison. I don't blame him; I don't think that would have ultimately been very fulfilling to me, even if it would have meant far less student-loan debt. Psychology was my primary focus, so I crossed my fingers, applied to a bunch of graduate school programs, and got accepted to a couple.

## GRAD SCHOOL

I thought I was going to do research, but when I dove into my master's-level clinical counseling psychology program, I discovered, thanks to their dual focus on clinical counseling and empirical research, that I actually loved therapy and kind of wanted to take a detour from the Ph.D. route to just work for a while and pay off some of my debt (having no idea what that would actually look like). The sun was setting on my deferment period as I closed in on graduation, and I knew those student loan servicers were going to come calling very soon.

Throughout all these natural next steps on the path to a career in psychology, I still wrestled with music, mostly internally. It sort of came to a head near the end of grad school though, when I found myself singing background vocals for an up-and-coming country artist who was gaining a lot of traction in the music industry. My husband, John, was playing bass for him, and I was suddenly swept up into this incredible dream come true, where I was singing harmonies (my favorite) to fun, catchy songs in bars, super-cool music venues in multiple states, and outdoor concerts in front of hundreds, maybe even thousands of people. John and I were actually having conversations during my last semester of grad school about the possibility of moving to Nashville to do this thing for real. Sadly, that never materialized. The artist we were backing got signed and we pretty much never heard from him again. That hurt a lot, because we were all friends, or so we thought, and there was no question we had been part of a killer band. For me, I think what hurt the most was suddenly being thrust into literal spotlights and then watching that dream evaporate just as quickly, for no apparent reason. Needless to say, my internal struggle with music was real and raw. We didn't move to Nashville; I finished my master's and settled into my new life as a professional counselor.

To some extent, my instincts to detour were right on. Practicing therapy (and going to my own therapy) changed and healed me in ways I couldn't have even grasped back when I was busy chickening out of music. As I made my way into a healthier version of myself, I realized that I had been catapulting myself from one extreme to the other, from rejecting music entirely to demanding (in my dreams) that music provided me ultimate fulfillment, pay my bills, and provide relief from my growing pile of student-loan debt. I regularly got lodged in steep valleys of regret. I couldn't keep catapulting; I couldn't keep it up, period.

## COVERED IN SPAGHETTI

So what does one do when she realizes something different needs to enter the equation, but has no idea what that something might be? She throws the whole pot of spaghetti at the walls. Burnout-combatting spaghetti: teaching undergraduate psychology classes; tutoring thesis writers and students of psychology, English, statistics, research methods, and data analysis; diving into continuing-education courses; slowing down her caseload and tinkering with specializations.

On top of these counseling-adjacent professional pursuits, I was doing everything I could think of in multiple attempts to balance the ongoing laundry-like cerebral work of therapy with tangible, finite, physically gratifying hobbies: cooking, sewing, and even building funky home decor out of old pianos and pump organ guts. I started reconnecting with my body and grounding myself with yoga and making stuff with my hands. I went to my own therapy. I got more involved at church. I found myself writing more and finally opening myself back up to music by writing songs again and eventually singing—even in public on a regular basis!

Some of this actually did curb the burnout, while some of it clarified what was going on when I noticed the burnout was lifting less and less. Self-care could only scrub so much of it off; the paths were diverging, and I was daydreaming of a parallel universe in which I actually had the guts and clarity to make a real change. Like I said, sometimes it takes me a long time to identify the problem. From there, it might still be a real trek to pursue a resolution. In my experience, that's been a painfully typical trajectory.

At some point in this process, I heard about a career coach who did excellent work. I'd actually referred a number of my own clients to her. I called her for a consultation, and being a former counselor herself, after about 20 minutes of hearing what was going on with me, she told me something profound about myself that I have never forgotten. She told me I sounded like an extrovert who recharges like an introvert (nail on head) and that I needed to be on the positive side of helping people, rather than down in the dark trenches of psychotherapy. This comment stuck with me because as soon as she said it, I knew she was completely right.

## BURNOUT

I had ridden the waves of burnout for a few years when I finally, consciously came to realize psychotherapeutic work was not going to be a lifelong career for me; at least, not a continuous one. It was not the only thing I would do. I was struggling a lot with feeling like my artistic endeavors would never have a chance, simply because I felt like I was way behind, not good enough to begin with, and unable to prioritize artistic creativity. My limited resources of time, energy, creativity, and joy were feeling increasingly scarce as the burnout cranked up.

Of course, I knew about burnout—I had received great training on this subject as part of my graduate school experience, and I have always been a doer, achiever, and hard worker, so I thought, okay, no problem! I'll just have to scale it back a bit. Except, there wasn't "no problem." In my view, there was a hundred-thousand-dollar problem: my student loan debt. It was hard for me to imagine scaling back my practice simply for "me" when my hour-by-hour sessions with clients (about whom I cared very deeply) also happened to be paying my bills. I couldn't take the hit to my income.

I'd somewhat monetized side hustles and hobbies before, but I had never before succeeded at making consistent, part-time income that I could count on to supplement a true reduction of my psychotherapy workload. I had already burned out of teaching at a university (boy, do I not miss lecturing for four hours at a time), wasn't interested in building a whole business of tutoring statistics work, editing theses, or data analysis consulting—so there I was, staring down the end of my psychology skill-set rope, wondering what else I could (or would allow myself to) do for money.

In the more intense moments of burnout, I was absolutely tortured by this feeling of stuckness. I was terrified that if I didn't do something soon, burnout would affect my work with my clients, for whom I wanted to be totally present and maximally effective. I was terrified of what people would think. I was disgusted with myself for abandoning my master's degree (which is exactly how I saw it for a long time). I had a real lie-down-in-the-bed-you've-made mentality. And you know what? It wasn't helpful. It wasn't healthy.

My close friends, family, and especially my husband, John, were all exasperated for me. I heard everything from "this too shall pass" to "start putting your resumé out there" and everything in between from very well-meaning people who loved me very much— all of whom had no more idea than I did about what my next move could or should be.

I felt lost, and I felt like it was all my fault. I chose the wrong career. I'm not cut out for this. I didn't realize how crushing and limiting my debt would be in real life, but I should have! I was stupid. I was naive. I should have known better. I was so disappointed in myself, and I was really scared that in spite of doing my very best to help people in the most obviously helpful profession I could think of, I was wasting my life being a counselor. There was so much missing, and I couldn't explain why—to myself or anyone else! I loved my clients. I loved working in private practice. I was a good therapist. Even considering all of that, I was thinking, "Is that all there is?"

This part of the conversation is always difficult for me, because I'm so wary of being misunderstood—especially regarding my clients. I was doing my very best to help each one of them, and I've always cared and carried out therapeutic work with deep conviction and respect for the human experiences I am privy to. It's an honor to walk with people in their most vulnerable moments. It's inspiring and amazing. In fact, I feel strongly that if a therapist or counselor does not regularly experience those things in their work with their clients, it's probably a sign that burnout is nigh. It's precisely because I have always cared so much about my clients that I was in such turmoil about making some kind of change. On one hand, I wanted to make sure my own personal existential struggle never affected any of them negatively in any way, directly or indirectly. On the other hand, I felt every single grain of sand as it slipped through the neck of the hourglass. Something had to change—really, really change.

## The Snag

I want to take a second here to name a specific snag that kept me stuck for a long time—like, years. When I was caught in it, I wasn't able to begin to entertain actually making a change; instead, I alternately soothed myself and swept it under the rug. That worked for a while. This was the snag: my own self-imposed expectation that my education had to pay for itself! Thank God I was talking to friends and family about this, because one person gave me some life-changing insight into this snag—and it blew the doors right off of my limited thinking.

One kind soul casually pointed out to me that over the course of my professional counseling career, my work technically had already netted more income than the amount of my outstanding debt. Blew. My. Mind. It sounds so simple now, but I was so frazzled about the burden of my debt that I had never once considered this. Of course, I still had a pile of debt because we used the money I'd made working as a counselor to pay a bunch of our household expenses and bills every month. Like ya do. John and I have both always worked really hard, but frankly, neither of us has ever individually made enough to pull off being a single-income household—ironically, this is largely due to having to make massive student loan payments every month. Even so, the realization that my degree could have, on paper, paid for itself freed me in a way. It opened my eyes and ears to the possibilities, and allowed me to then grapple with the humility of "abandoning" my master's degree. I mean, who does that?

## IDENTITY

Fortunately for me, when this eBay store came along, it didn't require a large financial risk, because I would never in a million years have entertained it if it had. However, it has required a few other kinds of risk along the way. The biggest one of all has been a risk of identity. Nobody calls me "Professor" or mistakes me for a doctor in this line of work—in fact, I think when people see me on the job, sourcing at a thrift store or something, they might make all kinds of other assumptions. If they see my tattoos, my gym clothes, my hours of free time in the middle of the day, my shopping cart piled high, I don't know exactly what assumptions would come out the other end of that equation, but I'd wager they're not as prestigious as the ones I used to get.

That's been a very salient new awareness for me, though—how much I cared if people knew (or assumed) I was smart, hardworking, educated, accomplished. I didn't think I cared too much about those things, but that was my perception from the position of enjoying the benefits of those assumptions. You can't read the label from inside the jar, right? Now I realize how much others' hypothetical opinions of me mattered to me, and how I now want those opinions to be of as little consequence to me as possible. This is a motive I'm inclined to check frequently, even as I'm writing this book.

Nothing has made me more aware of the identity-bound pressure we put on what we do than meeting new people in this season of my life. Sure, I can make the elevator pitch about being an online seller sound fun, mostly because it actually is fun, but it definitely doesn't land the same as introducing myself as a private practitioner psychotherapist and college professor.

There is actually some irony in the responses I get now versus then, which I find hilarious. As a therapist I often got some variation of these:

"Oh! Are you psychoanalyzing me? I, um, just remembered I have to be somewhere..."

"Oh! Man, my mother-in-law really needs some therapy! She is a real piece of work! You won't believe what she did on Tuesday..."

Nowadays, after mentioning the eBay store, I usually find myself immediately fielding tons of questions. It never ceases to amaze me how curious and energized people are when they ask me about the store. Not to mention, I love learning about people, and I am enjoying the freedom I have to share about my own life. It's no secret that "How do you do?" has been subtly replaced by "What do you do?" Even when I had an official career, this was hard to answer because I was always doing many things on my own time. In those introductory moments when I didn't want to put my therapist-foot forward first, I was always scrambling to find a way to elevator-pitch my current concoction of activities, because if I just tell someone I am one thing or do one thing, well, it feels a bit dishonest and one-dimensional. Now, I try to ask people when I meet them, "what are you into?" or "what have you been up to lately?" I'm not trying to knock the official career—I'm sure I'll have a predominant one again someday—but for the moment, I'm keen to focus on the 'who' rather than the 'do.'

If you haven't noticed, a lot of existential questions are woven into making any kind of life change. In my experience, that cannot be understated in cases of changing our lives in terms of what we do, perhaps especially what we do for a living. I've observed this in the lives of some of my clients, friends, family members, and not least of all, myself. In part, I think this is because we make decisions, commitments, and investments from a particular framework of who we are going to be, which to most of us, is interchangeable with what we are going to do, especially in moments of enrolling in college, starting training programs, declaring majors, applying for jobs or graduate school programs, and the like.

Even though my education was an extremely valuable experience, it came with a major unspoken assumption: if something didn't require a significant financial investment, it must not be too valuable. I didn't have money saved to pay for my education, so back then, I figured I was just going to have to commit now and pay for my investment along the way, like so many do. No big deal, right? It's unbelievable how much money I was allowed to borrow with nary a credit card, nor fully formed prefrontal cortex. I could have purchased a house with the amount of money I borrowed for my education, and I had scholarships, too! Believe me, thinking about this for too long starts to feel crushing.

I don't regret my path, largely because of my faith. On days when I've been way down in the valleys of regret and despair about my overwhelming student-loan debt (which, still to this day, requires a monthly payment that rivals my mortgage), I have been known to tell John, through tears and sometimes even snot, that I'd trade in all three of my degrees for the money back, right this instant. I was certainly well-educated in an academic sense, but I have felt so very, incredibly stupid and mislead. I have wanted to start over. I have felt like an easy target.

Many times, once my student-loan payments had kicked in (they were always more expensive than our rent), I would get angry and blame the lenders or adults in my life for not warning me, just to offload enough of the blame to be able to live with myself. I was the one who had signed on the line, after all. It's really scary to look back and realize that you made a huge, irrevocable decision and at the time, didn't detect even a slight shift in the breeze, not a hint of foreshadowing, not a shred of a red flag. It made me question everything and live small—for a while.

While I'm picking bones with societal expectations about college and student loans, I'd just like to say for the record that the adjacent pressure on young adults to hurry up and get situated is garbage! Experience is where it's at: experiencing things to know what your values really are, to know what a good fit really feels like, and to know not only what you are interested in, but how you are interested in functioning, being in the world, and spending your actual life.

I remember taking a career-values assessment in graduate school as part of our career counseling class. This exercise has always stuck with me, because it was so simple and I learned so much from it. There were at least 20 career values—I could have probably thought of five off the top of my head, but the other 15 or so were far less obvious, yet incredibly useful to consider. Career values are just aspects of work that might matter to you—things like high pay, vacation time, social interaction on the job, work environment, dynamic and challenging work, precision in your work, a flexible schedule, etc. The exercise we did in my class was to essentially prioritize a given set of career values, 1-20. This was the first time I realized the work environment was extremely important to me. In fact, I had worked in all kinds of environments, and finally realized during this exercise that the differences among them were what basically determined how much I liked or disliked or thrived in or quit each and every one of the jobs I'd ever had.

What great information! When I was deciding between some options for work after graduate school, I considered this information seriously. Working in a cozy office private practice setting was certainly the ideal work environment for me as a counselor. I knew enough about myself to know that. It was soothing and comfortable, with plenty of autonomy, meaningful work, flexibility, and decent pay. I really did feel like a spoiled brat for a while once I had admitted to myself that even in an ideal work environment, it wasn't a good enough fit for me to commit my whole working life. I felt for a long time like I should just shut up and accept that it's good enough, even if it's not great. Here was the problem: I knew it could be better, and now that I had experience to confirm my career values, I couldn't ignore what I had learned. I couldn't settle for good. And I couldn't make a change until I made some space.

## MAKING SPACE

There is so much more to starting an eBay store than clearing off a shelf in your garage and heading to the thrift shop with $20 in your pocket. I'll admit, Macklemore makes it look pretty dang fun, and it is fun. It's fun, it's gratifying, it's a little complicated at times. It's greater than the sum of its parts, and it requires some give and take. First you make space for it, and in return, it makes space for you.

The shift into this unapologetic, miscellaneous life didn't happen all at once, but it crystalized in the wake of tragedy that had abruptly punctuated a year and a half of experiencing incrementally more freedom. The desires requisite to fully shifting into a project-based lifestyle with eBay chugging along in the background already had been stirring simmering for a good while. A couple of the things I was most excited to engage with fully included creating music on my own, in my church community, and in the pop-rock duo of which I am half, Jasper + Jade.

The other half of Jasper + Jade, my ride-or-die friend, Katie Snyder. She and I also created a podcast that we host together called The Doing Scary Things Podcast, in which we talk about all kinds of stuff like this among ourselves and our guests. It actually started organically out of our own conversations as we worked together to pursue music, our joint scary thing! Katie is even writing a book and frequently working with clients in this area as a life-purpose coach.

As I sat down in a coffee shop, literally day one of fleshing out my skeletal book outline, writing this chapter and effectively starting my book for realsies, Katie sat next to me working on finishing her book. This coffee shop day was in January 2020—almost exactly a year after we got that dreadful call about my Aunt Patti, and for reasons both good and achingly sad, it now felt like a whole different life.

On one hand, Patti has really been gone for almost a year, and I can hardly even believe those words as I see them appear on my screen. On the other hand, realizing that something really had to change (read: a cartoon anvil of realization falling out of the sky straight onto my head) afforded me space—both for the sake of space itself, and for endeavors I believe to be the highest and best use of my life and myself. From making music and podcasting, to writing plays and musicals, to baking wedding cakes for my friends, to creating new mental health resources for an organization I cherish, to hanging out with my niece and nephew, to last-minute road trips, to enjoying coffee with John every morning, to rereading Harry Potter with Cinder snoozing away on my lap. To get to say "yes." To be allowed to say "no."

It's so fun to have eBay running parallel to all those things, supporting them, the way Elizabeth Gilbert talks about in Big Magic (it's a must-read—thanks forever for that one, Liz).

Making space for the things that matter most required me to make space for myself. Rather than cramming my square-peg self into a square-ish hole (almost fits, if you jam it really hard), I cut out a more angular, square place for myself to fit into with revelatory degrees of comfort and ease: a much better fit. The most important change here was structural—indeed, a shift to being project-based. I'm kind of binge-y at heart, and I get bored easily with many tasks the moment I feel stagnant. I like to move and make stuff and do stuff with my hands—and, of course, shop.

The nature of the cumulative, delayed-income model of the eBay store creates so much time for me to move and make and do—all while making money from work that I previously did. This also means I don't have to demand any kind of income from my creative projects—I might gently request it from them later, but they are all allowed as much time as they need to fully develop, pressure-free.

These days, I even entertain the idea of having actual hobbies again—saving some of this free time for domestic skills I enjoy, like sewing, gardening, cooking, and of course, rifling through countless long boxes for certain back issues of comic books with John. I'd love to spend my Saturdays doing any of those things, rather than working some more because I feel like I have to, or crashing from all the work I crammed into the previous week and painstakingly trying to recharge my batteries for the Monday around the corner.

## HOW'S IT GOING?

So far, so—so—good. I am amazed every day that there was actually a creative solution available to me—a way out of the system I felt totally trapped by. It's easy for me to confirm that it is, indeed, working. However, I have no intention of parking on eBay for the rest of my life and calling it a career. That was never the point. It's a catalyst, not a destination, but I'm loving the ride.

If I had stayed stuck, it would have been too easy to continue to blame other people, systems, and my past self for the situation I found myself in. That's what people do when they feel helpless; but blaming ourselves, or even assigning responsibility, is not the same as taking responsibility. Finding a way to make change happen was ultimately how I chose to take responsibility, and rather than condemning, it was freeing. It is freeing. I'm doing it. I'm paying off my debt. I'm creating more music. I'm writing a book, for Pete's sake! I'm holding space for new opportunities and possibilities. I'm letting go of those past perceptions of self, career, business, and adulting which proved to be unhelpful. Best of all, I encounter no life-or-death situations, no crises, no emergencies, and very few actual problems dealing with my online resale business.

Now don't get me wrong, I still have struggles, and my struggles are still valid, but they are very different struggles than the ones I had a year ago, and the ones I had three years ago, and the

157

ones I had seven years ago. My current struggles still run the gamut of good, bad, and ugly: daily exposure of the harsh judgements and unrealistic expectations I have for myself, working too much, finding and fine-tuning my sense of balance in about a hundred aspects of life.

I also enjoy some upsides I didn't used to have, at least not in full form, such as opportunities to be spontaneous, apply grace, and enjoy the moment. Learning curves abound, but I'm a pretty practiced learner at this point, so I'm okay with that. I still have plenty of moments of doubt—not helplessness or hopelessness, though. In those moments, I already know the remedy: put my head down and get some stuff listed—or just wait 24 hours and see if my doubt has lifted on its own. Many doubts have a much shorter lifespan than you'd think.

I've learned a lot about potential; mostly, I've learned to pay attention. It's important to be brutally honest about the reality of the current manifestation of whatever it is I'm after (mastery of a skill, self awareness, etc.) I must regularly take note of my reality, especially when I want to consider my potential. Potential is what drives me forward in a hopeful spirit; it tips me off to notice the small signs of progress that can sometimes be hard to see, even when I'm looking.

I've also learned a lot about capacity, and how much my perception of capacity can differ from the true capacity of something. I am curious: can capacity itself increase? Is there really always a growing edge? Maybe it's analogous to filing items away in my garage, which already seems packed. It's a challenge, especially when I am feeling excited and motivated, to figure out where my capacity is, what my growing edge is, and whether I want to operate at maximum capacity, and if so, for how long. This is true in my store as well as in my life.

I'm thinking a lot about capacity these days, as my everyday life and workflow are almost totally self-determined, self-directed, and self-motivated. That's a lot of self, and I'd be lying if I said I never get sick of my own company. (Try writing a book. Sheesh.) In all seriousness though, this is my life—the one that I've got—and I do want to make the most of it. I do want to spend it responsibly, meaningfully, and much to the joy of myself and others. I want to do what I was made to do. I want to invite everyone else to the party.

## GROW ON

On a nuts-and-bolts level in the eBay store, my lifestyle vehicle that leads the way to everything else, there are so many things I want to improve. Obviously, continuing to chip away at an even-larger and better inventory is key. That will involve decisions about hiring other people to help with different aspects of processing items, possibly expanding inventory storage somehow, and tangling with some of the nattering issues that are ever-present in the store today, such as finding a better way to store my shipping supplies, swapping out some of my crappy old storage bins for newer, better ones (preferably clear, so I can see the contents), and learning to use new back-end features of eBay as the platform continues to improve. Heck, I know I'm underutilizing the tools at my disposal as a seller that are already there, but I've put the vast majority of my time into building a large inventory and simplifying and refining the most-necessary systems first. It's served me well so far, but I may need to dig around on eBay one of these days to discover what else might be available to further streamline my business.

I have learned that there is plenty of room to improve on something that's already working, but to find yourself in the middle of something that's already working, you have to start! It's totally acceptable to work on perfecting it later, if you find that perfection still matters to you down the road. In my experience perfection always looks the most necessary before a project is off the ground, and nearly always turns out to be wildly overrated. I could pack stuff more nicely, I could probably source more efficiently or diversely, fine. Some improvements don't seem important to me, and I may never do them at all; other improvements I am definitely interested in exploring.

Before we go our separate ways, there is something I want to confess to you. For a long time, without even realizing it, I perceived miscellaneous as negative. In the most neutral sense, what that word indicated was the category to which all the things that don't belong anywhere else would inevitably go. Like the Island of Misfit Toys. Those "things" typically included the complicated stuff that we can't be bothered to figure or categorize—the weird stuff, the random stuff. The thing is, I relate to that stuff. I didn't know it was possible to embrace all those parts and pieces; I thought the only thing you could do with them was dump them in a miscellaneous bin for a rainy day. Or to deal with later. Or to deal with never.

When I was younger, I even felt suspicious of my friends who were into whatever I subjectively (and often unconsciously) deemed to be "too many things" and even worse, I judged my friends for it. They can't possibly really be good at so many things at once, or committed and loyal to so many things at once, or actually be doing their best and giving their all to so many things at once. Obviously, I'd never heard the term "multi passionate" before, and if I had, I'd probably have scoffed at it. Maybe that's where you are right now. That's ok; the meaning of "multi passionate" has certainly been worn until threadbare in some circles, and it might even make your eyes feel rolly. I get that. I was fortunate enough to be introduced to this term by my awesome friend, Meg who happens to host *The Couragemakers Podcast* and *The Daily Pep*—she explained it in a very non-cringey way that I related to, deeply.

Truthfully, I think when it comes to our lives, resumes, and profiles, we are biased against the miscellaneous. Sure, we want to present all the right extracurriculars, certifications, volunteer experience—presenting that way makes us look like poster children for variety, the spice of life. Still, a diverse resume isn't the same as miscellaneous. The accomplished candidate is cultured, well rounded; the miscellaneous is . . . messy. There's certainly lots to be said for niches, specialization, commitment, and calling. But what's the difference between following curiosity and getting distracted by nonsense? If I'm a Jack-of-all-trades, I'm doomed to be a master of none. I'm not buying that anymore; a bias looks like the truth until you see the truth, then suddenly the bias looks like a bias. I've always been a little on the miscellaneous side; I still am, but now I know it by its real name, and I can understand it without the unnecessary and unfair connotations.

One thing I love about my eBay store as the foundation of the other ways I get to choose to spend my life, if I may borrow the verbiage from my little sister (thanks, MJ), is the revolving door of relearning the merits of being a beginner: the thrill of novelty, freedom to fail, fascination, being wrong, and the associated humility, to name a few. Affording (with time and money) this miscellaneous life means I get to revisit and deepen each of those merits, many times over.

So, the final question remains: is it working? Yes. Do I finally know what I'm doing now? No. Do I still enjoy regular helpings of humble pie? Sometimes, I even have seconds. My life is more miscellaneous than ever—and that's exactly how I want it to be.

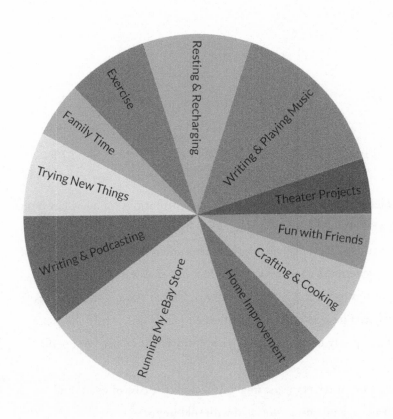

# APPENDIX

## OPERATIONAL DEFINITIONS & GRAINS OF SALT

Here are my own personal operational definitions for a few key terms as they apply to my store and charts throughout this book. If you have a business degree, forgive me for potentially bastardizing any of these terms. I wrote about them in a way that was true to how I conceptualize and apply them in real life as I run my store. This is where I have to confess that although I am a little nerdy about data, I'm a pretty basic data nerd. It's nothing fancy. It's far from perfect.

Net Profit refers to the total sales minus the cost of goods and necessary expenses associated with sold items.

Necessary Expenses include eBay fees, PayPal fees, shipping cost, and sales tax.

The Reinvestment category, should it be included in a chart here and there, includes things I choose to spend some of my profit on to reinvest in the store in an elective way, such as new inventory, additional shipping and storage. supplies, etc. I don't lump these kinds of things in with Necessary Expenses to keep it simple, and because Reinvestment is a wildly variable and frankly less-necessary category. Those expenses are still beneficial to the business as a whole, but not required in the way that eBay and PayPal fees, sales tax, and shipping costs are. That's just how I like to think about it, so there.

Consignment costs are not factored in for the sake of simplicity, but generally I keep 50% of the profit from consignment items (which are few and far between, anyway). Fees and other expenses are not factored in either, because I'm basically interested in: 1. How much did I pay for this, and 2. How much was someone willing to pay for it online? It's a given in my mind that there are associated fees with each item/running the store in general.

# Resources and Mentions

## Good Listens

- Scavengerlife.com and The Scavenger Life Podcast
- Affordanything.com and the Afford Anything Podcast with Paula Pant
- www.katiesnyder.com and The Doing Scary Things Podcast
- www.thathummingbirdlife.com and The Daily Pep and The Couragemakers Podcast
- Jasper + Jade music available wherever you listen to music

## Good Reads

- Big Magic by Elizabeth Gilbert
- Secondhand by Adam Minter

## eBay Store Resources

- Ebay.com
- Paypal.com
- Usps.com

## Total Cost of Goods by Source

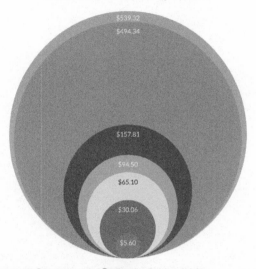

$539.32
$494.34
$157.81
$94.50
$65.10
$30.06
$5.60

● eBay (2.17%)  ● Estate Sales (4.69%)  ● Independent Thrift Shops (6.81%)
● For-Profit Thrift Shops (38.89%) ● Nonprofit Chain Thrift Shops (35.65%) ● Retail Arbitrage (0.4%)
● Yardsales (11.38%)

## Profit Margin by Source

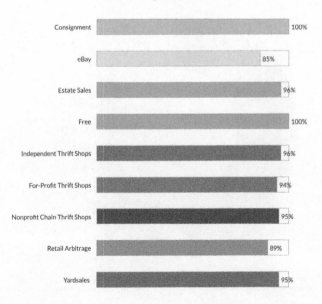

| Source | Margin |
|---|---|
| Consignment | 100% |
| eBay | 85% |
| Estate Sales | 96% |
| Free | 100% |
| Independent Thrift Shops | 96% |
| For-Profit Thrift Shops | 94% |
| Nonprofit Chain Thrift Shops | 95% |
| Retail Arbitrage | 89% |
| Yardsales | 95% |

## Sales by Category 2017-2020

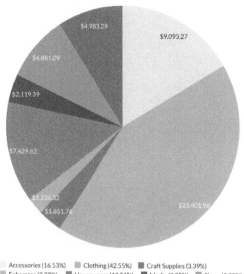

Accessories (16.53%)   Clothing (42.55%)   Craft Supplies (3.39%)
Ephemera (2.23%)   Housewares (13.51%)   Media (3.85%)   Shoes (8.88%)
Toys & Collectibles (9.06%)

## 2017 Items Sold by Category

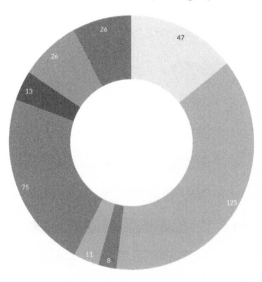

Accessories (14.2%)   Clothing (37.76%)   Craft Supplies (2.42%)   Ephemera (3.32%)
Housewares (22.66%)   Media (3.93%)   Shoes (7.85%)   Toys & Collectibles (7.85%)

## 2020 Items Sold by Category

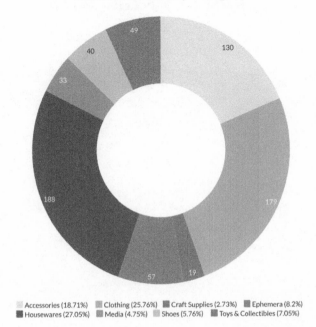

Accessories (18.71%) ■ Clothing (25.76%) ■ Craft Supplies (2.73%) ■ Ephemera (8.2%)
■ Housewares (27.05%) ■ Media (4.75%) ■ Shoes (5.76%) ■ Toys & Collectibles (7.05%)

## Average Sale 2017 / 2020 Category Comparison

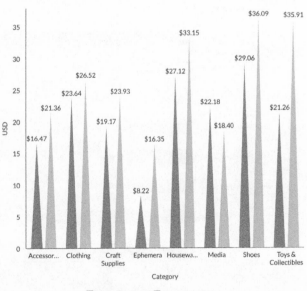

Average Sale 2017 ■ Average Sale 2020

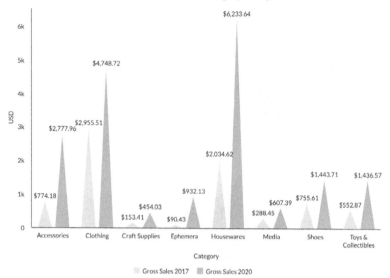

Gross Sales 2017 / 2020 Category Comparison

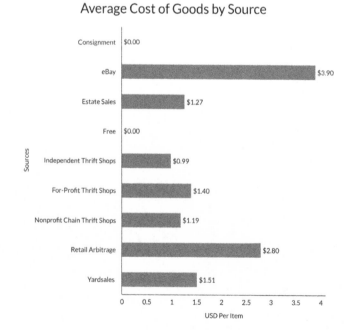

Average Cost of Goods by Source

## Items Sold by Source

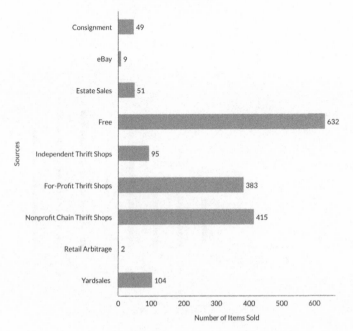

## Gross Sales by Source

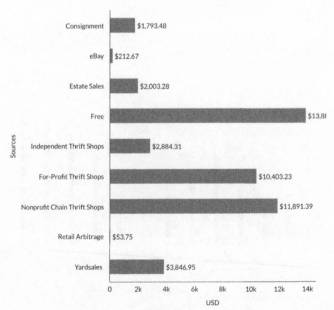

## 2017 Gross, Necessary Expenses, & Net

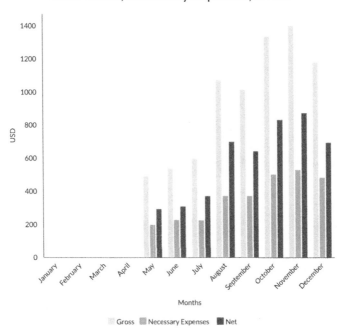

## 2018 Gross, Necessary Expenses, & Net

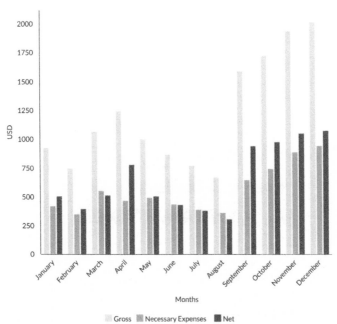

## 2019 Gross, Necessary Expenses, & Net

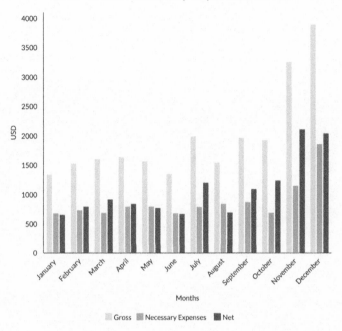

Made in the USA
Monee, IL
31 October 2020

46482068R00100